SCIENTIFIC HUMANISM AND CHRISTIAN THOUGHT

SCIENTIFIC HUMANISM
and
CHRISTIAN THOUGHT

by
D. DUBARLE, O.P.

Translated by
REGINALD TREVETT

1956
BLACKFRIARS PUBLICATIONS
LONDON

First Published in French under the title
HUMANISME SCIENTIFIQUE ET RAISON CHRÉTIENNE

by

Desclée de Brouwer, Paris

First Published in English 1956

Nihil Obstat: HUBERTUS RICHARDS, S.T.L., L.S.S.
Censor Deputatus.
Imprimatur: E. MORROGH BERNARD,
Vic. Gen.
Westmonasterii, die 3a OCTOBRIS, 1955

*Printed in Great Britain
at the* BURLEIGH PRESS, *Lewins Mead,* BRISTOL

CONTENTS

		Page
Foreword	. . . . . .	vii
Chapter 1.	Technics and the Future . . .	1
Chapter 2.	Present-Day Scientific Ideas and the Control of Human Situations	26
Chapter 3.	New Techniques and the Future of Mankind	52
Chapter 4.	The Universe of Science and Philosophy .	67
Chapter 5.	The Attitude of Christianity to Scientific Progress	93

FOREWORD

IT will be obvious that the five chapters of this essay were not written in sequence. They bring together with such slight modifications as were necessary the text of articles published and lectures delivered over the past few years. Hence there are repetitions and other defects for which I apologize. I have decided to allow them to remain so that the following pages may retain their character as an essay. Neither the general title nor the arrangement in chapter form should suggest that they are anything else. All I hope is that by placing these fragments side by side, I may make the various aspects of the human problem of science easier to grasp and enable Christian thought to adjust itself more adequately to the problems it raises.

The union of Christian thought and scientific humanism is an aim far beyond the slender achievements in that direction here offered to the reader. Nevertheless, if the considerations we have outlined do something towards furthering that aim, they will have amply fulfilled my purpose in committing them to writing. But even that is doubtless too ambitious a hope.

The last chapter, *The Attitude of Christianity to Scientific Progress*, was, as it happens, the first to be written. If I remember rightly, it was in 1947 that E. Mounier asked me to write it for a collection of papers in the "*Esprit*" series which did not in fact materialize. I published it eventually in the review "*Esprit*" in September, 1951. The first of the five chapters, *Technics and the Future*, appeared as an article in the February, 1950, issue of *La Vie Intellectuelle*. The second, *Present-day Scientific Ideas and the Control of Human Situations*, forms part of a symposium on Cybernetics published by Mounier in *Esprit* (October, 1950). The third, *New Techniques and the Future of Mankind*, is the text of a paper read in October, 1950, to the Madrid Congress for Intellectual Co-operation. Finally, the fourth, *The Universe of Science and Philosophy*, is, with slight alterations, the text of a lecture given at the Sorbonne in March, 1952, to conclude a series organized by the Maison des Sciences on the theme "Scientific Thought and the Structure of the Universe." I offer my sincere thanks to all who have given permission for these articles and papers to be used in the present book.

Paris, April 15th, 1953.

CHAPTER I

TECHNICS AND THE FUTURE

Towards a Science of Anticipation

NOTHING perhaps is more important for the future of mankind than an intelligent anticipation of future technical developments. The history of the past two centuries clearly shows that, if all is to be well, it is not enough to discover new ways of exploiting natural resources and then to allow men to use the powers thus acquired as they wish, with every individual or group left free to turn them to what seems at the moment to be the best account. With the passage of time such an irresponsible attitude towards industrial developments resulting from new technical processes, has proved inadequate and dangerous, not only because man is not wholly good and often applies the means at his command to evil ends, but also and perhaps principally because the utilization of the technical resources he has mastered inevitably affects the rest of his life and produces various by-products of the result he had in mind. These by-products may be extremely important and often undesirable. If wholly unchecked, they may become chronic evils and more than counterbalance the hoped-for benefits which have inspired the efforts made.

Thus those who foresaw the initial rise of mechanized industry emphasized the prosperity in store for mankind. They were quite right, but very few of them seem to have realized that by bringing into being a world of crude machinery and by uncritically allowing full play to the norms of a profit-making economy, they were inevitably moving towards the creation of a proletariat,

Industry in its early stages made inevitable the reduction of the workers to a servile status, and the harsh economic point of view adopted by big business inevitably meant that the labouring masses were looked upon as a means of production tied to the machine by a kind of natural law. In the world of to-day we grow increasingly aware of the painful disadvantages which accompany the very considerable growth of general prosperity among the nations that have followed the path of industrial civilization.

Numerous other implications might be mentioned. They all have this in common, that they were not foreseen at the outset. In retrospect they do not seem so difficult to discern as they in fact were to minds ill prepared to take note of them. In the light of subsequent developments we are now able to see in the circumstances and human events of two centuries ago, the logical causes of the facts which have emerged right down to our times. But it is equally clear to us that if men had reflected more and at the right time, they would have been able to see not only the possibilities which have been actualized but also other equally possible lines of development. They would then have been able to exercise their power of choice, instead of finding themselves unwittingly subjected to the laws of that fate which now threatens our future with so many perils.

But we, in our turn, still have time to engage successfully in reflexions similar to those we criticize our predecessors for having largely failed to make. New technical inventions as important, to say the least, as those we owe to the past, are now being perfected. It is clearly obvious that they cannot be left for mankind to do with them whatever it chances to judge fit. This revival of the philosophical liberalism of two centuries ago is no longer conceivable. It would be tantamount to-day to an abdication of the mind. Moralists and novelists seem to give us a useful lesson in this respect. The former emphasize our present bitter disillusionment with a society launched too uncritically along the path of exclusively material progress, whilst the latter are filled with forebodings as they foresee the future state of a world shaped by our present achievements. The great inventions of man's genius are real events in his history. He now experiences an urgent need to react to them in a new way.

But the problem must be approached not only from the standpoint of the educator and the moralist, but also from a standpoint more akin to that of the natural scientist, who is convinced that many aspects of man's being are to be studied, all other things being equal, in the same way as is a physical body. It is also necessary to give, as far as possible, a more precise and scientific form to the visions of the future which men of letters seek in the spontaneous outpourings of the imagination. In short, the time has come for us to concern ourselves with the search for a genuinely rational discipline which shall devote itself to the analysis of the future possibilities we carry within us. Neither formless poetical myths nor vague moral generosity are sufficient any longer in such serious matters.

We must be even more precise when we confront the moralists who find themselves at odds with the problems of technical progress. We are certainly not calling into question the value of their efforts. It is always necessary to awaken in man a high sense of his dignity and still more a profound respect for that of his neighbour. It is better still to strive to make men more receptive to the law of love which it is the purpose of the Gospel to promulgate. Diagnoses made from this point of view and condemnations uttered in the name of these demands are not to be set aside. Yet it must be realized that diagnoses of this type, condemnations of our failures and exhortations to more virtuous conduct are not enough. At the root of it all there is also a problem in human physics which cannot be evaded.

In practice what always seems to happen is that new discoveries, once their principles have been established, react upon the total mass of humanity to produce the future. These mutual reactions should not be considered as trivial nor as determined. They depend—and this is the physicist's concern—on the nature of the discoveries and on the state of the "mass" of human existence with which the reaction will take place. It would seem that several different possibilities are involved. A carefully elaborated physics might at least tell us something about them, and it would be for man to give his verdict for or against. Then the attitudes of mind with which the moralist is concerned, would find useful employment.

Doubtless, the science of these mutual reactions still has, in the main, to be built up, at least to the degree of reliability which modern science aims to achieve in all its forms. True, we have for the first time reached a stage at which it seems of vital importance that we should be successful. For the means by which man has progressed in the past—agriculture, the domestication of animals, fire, tools, and even the machines of the past few centuries, had only a limited power of reaction upon the mass of humanity. The contents of Pandora's box could be allowed to escape, and the results they automatically produced were not too deadly (even though they were so to a certain degree) for the race of mankind whose level of awareness is low and whose spirit never rises above the mediocre. Perhaps after all, even laissez-faire has been more profitable hitherto than any other attitude. On the other hand, man to-day foresees that of all the possibilities open to him, the worst is probably that to which he would be led by intellectual sloth. Knowledge is possible and we must attempt to acquire it. Otherwise the moral aspirations of conscience will remain in a state of flux or become involved in circumstances whose play and true character have not been discovered by the intellect. By a further irony of fate, the path to that future hell with which contemporary moralists vie with each other in threatening our sinful civilization, runs the risk of being paved in fact with all the good intentions and with the effects of the fine speeches, which so easily satisfy our generation in the person of its moralists.

Present-day progress and war

Unfortunately, we must for the moment give up all idea of any real and serious science in the sphere of which we have just caught a glimpse. As once Plato was ashamed of the narrow range of mathematical knowledge in the Greece of his day, so we can only be ashamed at our inability to engage in an intellectual task which henceforth will be essential. Then we may tentatively put forward a few rough outlines to direct rather than to satisfy our thought.

From the technical standpoint, the present epoch is clearly creative to a phenomenal degree. The notes which follow are not intended in any sense to consider all our technical achievements nor even to enumerate those which seem most important for the future. They will deal specifically with only two of them, the discovery of nuclear energy and the systematic construction of self-regulating machinery. Everybody's attention has been drawn to the first of these by the atom bomb. The second is less spectacular at first sight. Eventually it may well prove the more important of the two. One thing is certain, its military importance is already to all appearances as decisive as that of the bomb. The English owe largely to radar their victorious resistance to threats of German invasion during the last war. On the technical level, the next war—if there is to be one—will probably be decided by superiority in automatically controlled machines.

But we have no intention here of leading up to a discussion between military experts. Yet it is essential to reflect on the fact that warfare is, in our times, the point of interaction between the recent achievements of man's technical genius and that mass of human existence which cannot possibly be set aside. Whether we like it or not, the bomb was the first considerable result of the technical exploitation of the possibilities revealed to man by the science of nuclear reactions. Similarly, whether we like it or not, military requirements may well be the most powerful stimulus to the considerable progress now being made in the sphere of automatic control. The notion of warfare waged with machines set in motion by the mere pressing of a button is certainly quite false. Nevertheless it remains a guiding idea. Enterprises resulting from recent technical progress therefore present a picture strikingly different from the peaceful industrial enterprises of two centuries ago. Such a difference doubtless presents many problems to the human science we have in mind. But it presents at the same time a specifically philosophical problem which a more strictly scientific analysis cannot neglect if it is to achieve any equilibrium in its own processes.

We are emerging from a period in which two postulates were maintained in our thought, whether implicitly or explicitly. On the one hand, no one doubted that science and technics would give access to material resources naturally destined to be of service to man in his inventions. Any unfortunate or destructive results were considered as merely secondary. Heat, steam, electricity, chemical forces, all were in themselves beneficial. At first sight at least, it was confidently assumed that there was a pre-established harmony between the physical world now open to technics and the world of man. On the other hand, men believed in a kind of spontaneous goodness in the race as a whole rather than in the moral goodness of the individual, formed as he was by the civilizing forces already in operation. Human nature, it was said, is fundamentally good. At least in its immediate effects, the interaction between human nature and the principles placed at man's disposal by technical achievements could only give good results. From the classical period onwards, the implicit philosophy of the promoters and users of technics held that the shadows in the picture were of merely secondary importance.

It would be dishonest to think that the facts as we now know them can all be easily fitted into this philosophy. We have already criticized its terribly meagre intellectual content in our opening paragraph. It is a fact that scientific discovery and technical progress, however honestly they have been pursued and with aims quite other than destruction, have nevertheless brought to the surface a terribly destructive force long before their constructive and, humanly speaking, beneficial powers have succeeded in appearing. This is so in the last analysis, not because of the endemic evil in man's nature, but because of the nature of nuclear phenomena in themselves. It is equally difficult for us to adapt our thought to their reality and to pursue our activities in their sphere.

The difficulties we have to face in our conquest of the universe are therefore more hard to imagine than the classical mind supposed in its most bitter moments of disillusionment. We call into question the doctrine of a pre-established harmony between man and the physical universe, at least outside of an area relatively limited to the primary elements of our experience and life. Nor is there any reason to suppose we may always count on a state of goodness in human nature so fundamental that it can never be corrupted or compromised. Without adopting a diametrically opposite view or dogmatically asserting that man is naturally wicked, we must nevertheless ask ourselves whether mankind in the mass is not subject to variations of polarity in this respect. The ancient philosophers in their reflexions on the evolution of cities and their institutions had already caught a glimpse of something of the kind. Although there is no effective method of measuring such alternations between good and evil, yet the notion that they are at least possible, may serve to make us more prudent when we engage in the thinking which is so important if wise policies are to determine our future. After all it is not a bad thing to remind ourselves that, because of the unhappy state of mankind in our day, we run the risk of seeing the most valuable achievements of the mind dragged down into the whirlpool of evil; to remind ourselves also that one of the problems of the age is to attempt to overthrow by methods other than those of technics, those collective polarities whose results are disastrous. There may well be a law of opposites in accordance with which a human project inaugurated with full awareness of possible evils and in fear of the worst, might ultimately prove more beneficial and fruitful than progress begun under the illusion that only good can result and with no understanding of the problems involved.

It is surely just as dishonest and stupid to adopt without more ado doctrines of despair, as though we were hypnotized by the rising tide of fear which is all the present has to offer to so many. One of the most necessary tasks in our times is to provide a reasonable evaluation of the present situation of mankind, unequal as it is to the means it now has at its disposal.[1]

For this evaluation it is perhaps necessary to remember first of all that the link between warfare and technics is far from being a new thing. It has had far from negligible consequences in the past. In point of fact, it has been responsible for many of the characteristics of mankind to-day. But we have habitually refused to see it as the principal link between the fact of technical invention and human organization. Nor did we ever imagine that this link might eventually become a question of life or death for the human

[1] In all that follows, the war potential of mankind to-day is always considered only as one of the terms in the present situation which we must attempt to evaluate. There are many others and we are not attempting to give anything like a complete picture.

race, or at least for the whole of one type of civilization. Mind and humanity, so we thought, were united for peace and its pursuits. War indeed was responsible for many disasters and deaths, yet we agreed to treat such disasters and deaths as *incidental* evils since for fifteen centuries they had done little to deflect the onward march of Western man. To-day, although the achievements inherited from the past have been scarcely affected, yet war seems to have become the predominant factor in the case of the most recent technical inventions, and this at precisely the time when the destructive forces available are so powerful that they threaten if not the existence of the whole human race at least the permanence of its normal structures. We have come to realize the essential impermanence of what a short while ago we thought was indestructible. And not only this, but many of us frankly confess that we see the likelihood of catastrophe more clearly than the means by which our survival, improbable as it is, can be secured.

There is no reason to suppose that this view is entirely justified or that the traditional links have been so completely reversed. Perhaps we are inclined to over-dramatize the anxiety we feel. We will not attempt to discuss this point for the moment. In the absence of any satisfactory method of approach to an objective judgment, we must accept the fact that there is a disconcerting variety of opinions based on anything but genuine evidence. On the other hand, it is more important to see that our analysis should deal with possibilities of every kind.

In this connection, the short term importance of the links between more recent technical advances and man's preparations for war, is almost too obvious. There can be no question but that it is uppermost in the minds of our modern war lords. Nothing is more noteworthy than the care with which every effort is now being made to determine beforehand the dates in the armaments race programme. ' In 195 . . we shall have such and such equipment, but by then the enemy will have succeeded in establishing such and such a war potential . . . etc.' The importance of these facts may be decisive at any moment in the near future, if by any chance another war gives the new technical factors in our world the opportunity of combining together, if not for the total extermination of mankind—which still seems very unlikely—at least for the all but absolute destruction of our civilization—an event much easier to imagine.

But we must note that, whatever the outcome of future events may be, the repercussions of the present link between technics and war will have their effect upon the state of the human race as a whole. It is this state which is likely to be thrown into confusion and so present henceforward quite a different set of concrete circumstances in which mankind and technical progress will interact upon one another. We do not imply that the ultimate possibilities of such interaction will be abolished. Sooner or later, relations interrupted by possible future catastrophes will inevitably be renewed, though perhaps on a different footing. The ancient world was overwhelmed by the Romans and the barbarians, and many centuries elapsed before men could advance further along the line of rational inquiry inaugurated by the Greeks. Yet, with resources far more slender than ours, the mind of man took up the thread again at the very point where the Greeks had allowed it to be lost. We cannot believe that anything can ever permanently destroy a factor so enduring in the life of man.

Under no circumstances, therefore, can we be dispensed from looking beyond the short to the long term significance of present developments. On a long term view and even taking into account the ultimate bearing of the immediate situation on our human destiny, the military significance of the present technical advances will most probably turn out to be of secondary importance, in spite of the crucial problems such advances will force us to face.

On the other hand, the peaceful exploitation (and by this we do not necessarily mean a successful and healthy exploitation) of the new resources has every chance of becoming increasingly important in its results, and its effects upon mankind will be far more numerous in proportion, than those produced by the advent of machines in the artisan world of the eighteenth century. Here again our analyses may well prove ludicrously superficial. Before we attempt to make them, we must warn the reader that a far more ambitious effort would be required in order to satisfy the demands of a true scientific outlook. For the moment we can do no more than offer a few very inadequate introductory remarks.

Present possibilities and their peaceful development

We will avoid generalizations and come straight to the point of the questions before us. During the first decade since its discovery, nuclear energy has proved somewhat difficult for man to handle as a source of power. Its scope, all but infinite in theory, is thus considerably reduced in practice. One gramme of matter converted into energy would be sufficient to supply the Paris area—industrial and private consumption combined—with its present weekly requirements in kilowatts. But the conversion of heavy matter into energy still needs elements which are extracted with difficulty by costly metallurgical processes. Complicated apparatus has to be devised and then only a minute fraction of the mass of the material used can be converted. Further, we have to be content to recover this energy in its most elementary form as heat at a relatively low temperature of a few hundred degrees at the most. Finally, steps have to be taken to obviate the inconveniences due to the liberation of considerable and highly dangerous radioactivity at the same time as the energy itself is recovered. Radioactivity is a by-product of importance in many respects, but it calls for a large number of safety appliances. When all these material handicaps are taken into account, it seems that atomic power stations will have to be, in the immediate future at least, heavy industrial plants, just able to compete with other available sources of energy, such as steam generating stations, dams, etc. But we must ask ourselves how soon this situation is likely to change. At present, nuclear energy, though offering a possible contribution to industrial requirements, seems to have relatively few advantages. Yet there is nothing to stop us thinking that we are still at a crude, primitive stage in our exploitation of the new potentialities. Indeed, it seems most likely that nuclear energy will tend to overtake the usual sources of motive power in our times, and to replace them when necessary. It is even possible that as it takes over from them, it may bring about profound changes in industrial methods, by placing at man's disposal, under increasingly easy conditions, quantities of energy incomparably greater than those required by the machines of our present civilization.

Both the absolute value the new source of power is destined to assume, and its value in relation to the other sources of energy, will have a determining effect on many spheres of human life. Moreover, the speed at which the change-over takes place is a matter of vital importance. For if we are fast moving towards a radical transformation in the scale of the sources of energy available to us, this too rapid revolution may have incalculable and, in the long run, disastrous results, far more disastrous even than those of the atomic bomb. It would obviously be premature to risk any precise forecast as to the rate of expansion introduced into the field of energy sources by the new discoveries. Nevertheless, we should perhaps be well advised to estimate that, as things now are, we have little more than a century of peaceful work ahead of us, before we find ourselves in the presence of a factor which will change not merely the scale of the industrial problem, but its specific nature. What, we may ask, will the world be like when man has succeeded in utilizing sources of energy sufficient to satisfy all needs at a negligible cost?

The significance of the achievements now made possible by the progress of nuclear physics is easier to explain than that of the automatic regulation techniques. We shall try, however, to give some idea of the importance of these techniques by making some preliminary observations as to their purpose. We are all familiar with certain automatically functioning machines in common use, for instance, the escalator which is set in motion by the user as he moves towards the lowest step. On his way he intercepts a pencil of light rays directed onto a photo-electric cell. The impulse generated in the photo-electric cell by the resultant variation in the light, is sufficient, after adequate amplification, to set the whole apparatus in motion. Present-day industry is bringing into use an increasing number of such machines. In the Paris cinemas, a recent film gave a demonstration of automatic machines whose successive operations were controlled by cams regulating the working of each of the separate parts of the system. These machines operate without any human agency, solely by combining the time and movement factors of the mechanism according to a scheme worked out beforehand and suited to the manufacture of the desired product. The economical and efficient mass-production of many types of implement is thus made possible.

But in a machine there is much else which can be regulated besides the time and movement factors of certain of its parts, for example, speeds, such as that of the revolutions of a motor; temperatures, such as that of an electrolytic bath; the voltage of a circuit . . . and so on indefinitely. Further, it is possible to arrange for some regulating processes to be brought into play by the machine itself, instead of being, in a sense, imposed upon it from outside, as is the case when they are written beforehand into the design of the cams which guide the running of the different parts of the mechanism. With this end in view, the machine is fitted with a piece of apparatus capable, up to a point, of detecting faults in the working, and of correcting these by reacting on the factors involved in the functioning itself of the mechanism. Servo-mechanisms of every kind are the result.

The construction of servo-mechanisms leads in its turn to an idea of very general application: it is possible to make a process produce an intentionally pre-determined effect, and if necessary in a way quite independent of the actual purposes of the process under consideration. For instance, an aeroplane in flight moving towards a target determined by the pilot, can be detected and located by the acoustical apparatus or the radar of an anti-aircraft battery. The information collected by this detector equipment can be transmitted to an automatic laying apparatus, which will make it possible for the battery to fire a shell at the required point in the estimated trajectory of the plane. All this could be done if necessary without any human agency. The plane which is being attacked is thus transformed, in spite of itself, by the anti-aircraft equipment, into an integral part of a circuit of mechanical relations, whose outcome is the destruction of the plane. Although there are very obvious differences, this circuit of relations is fundamentally similar to the circuit operating in a servo-mechanism. The plane here provides the basic events which cause the circuit to function. The battery equipment, from the radar to the salvos of shells bursting at a given point in space, forms the machine for the production of an effect planned to take place when these events are realized.

This is only one example and the general theory of regulations can offer an astonishing variety of others. They all suggest the amazing possibility that the behaviour of certain kinds of apparatus may be compared to the reflexes of human beings. The analogies are so striking that the theorists of these mechanical regulations are always on the look-out for what they consider instructive comparisons between the functioning of the apparatus they devise and that of the nervous system by means of which a living organism can produce its various reactions.

It must be admitted that the production of even a far from perfect regulation system by means of purely mechanical devices, meets with many difficult problems, as is clearly shown by the example of the anti-aircraft unit. The solution of problems of speed and precision often requires delicate and extraordinarily expensive equipment. But, above all, as soon as the problems presented to the machine are at all complex, either because of the character of the initial data or because of the elaborate demands that have to be met if an adequate answer is to be forthcoming, it is necessary to assemble machinery so complex in itself, that we find the task beyond our powers. If the central control of an artillery battery is to be equal to the difficulties inherent in the problem it is called upon to solve, it would have to be an extremely complicated piece of apparatus. It can only be produced at present in relatively crude and simplified forms.

However, the automatic control centres which may shortly provide the solution to the regulation problems we are now beginning to formulate, are already foreshadowed by the great modern calculating machines. Thanks to the latter, as we know, it is possible to perform with speed and relative ease calculations required for numerical answers to certain mathematical problems—calculations so vast as to be beyond our human powers. These 'electronic brains' rudimentary as they still are, help us to foresee a whole series of similar devices for all kinds of purposes. It will be possible to connect them in many different ways to two pieces of apparatus, one of which will be able to explore the concrete facts, whilst the other will control effectors of every type. These machines are still in their infancy and of so novel a kind that it is difficult to set, even now, any limit to their powers.

We may therefore see the development of an entirely new machinery whose possibilities may radically alter the shape of things to come. These possibilities are of two kinds at least. In the first place they concern our present industrial machinery. There is already a movement on foot which tends to substitute to an increasing extent automatic regulation for human control of the machines we have inherited from the past. In the carrying out of his industrial tasks man will find himself resorting more and more to the use of a new mechanical medium, capable of abolishing to a large extent the subhuman character and the wasteful dispersal of the labour inevitable in industry while still in its primitive stages.

The second group of possibilities arises from the application of theories of regulation to human affairs, demographic, economic, sociological and even cultural. It seems that it will eventually be possible to achieve such a degree of knowledge of certain collective phenomena that automatic regulation of human reactions will be brought about by methods similar to those which open the way to the automatic regulation of machinery. It is true that we are far from possessing this power, but there is nothing absurd in imagining that one day we shall master it. We must therefore envisage the eventual rise of a new type of industry hitherto unknown, an industry which will procure for us a precise knowledge and perhaps also the regulation of those human processes whose detailed analysis is beyond the "artisan" level of the powers of our human brain. One thing at least is beyond question, the now certain invention of a new mechanical equipment for enlarging our knowledge will produce considerable changes in certain aspects of science. Even mathematics, which seem to be the branch of knowledge least dependent upon circumstances, may see their practice and general direction greatly modified by the introduction of mechanical aids to mental work.

Here again it is probably too soon to estimate the rate of

development and to say how far circumstances in the near or distant future will bring their influence to bear in an opposite direction. Yet, once more, there is nothing absurd in thinking that—unless extraneous causes ruthlessly intervene—only a few generations of human labour separate us from an epoch in which the majority of industrial tasks will only be performed by man through the medium of automatic regulations of a highly complex structure. Nor is it absurd to foresee—though apparently only on condition that the human mind contributes an immense inventive effort—that only a short period of time separates us from the day when men will possess a whole network of industrial plant for the acquisition of knowledge and perhaps also for the automatic regulation of human affairs. As in the case of the conquest of nuclear energy, it may well be that the results obtained will be so important that they will be not only a factor introducing a variation in the scale of the industrial problem or of other human problems, but also the source of a radical change in the very nature of these problems. What kind of world should we have, for instance, if man succeeded in making the production and distribution of the necessities of life an automatic process?

What will the World of the future be like?

The prospects we suggested by way of conclusion to what we have just written concerning nuclear energy on the one hand and automatic regulations on the other, can now be compared. In making this comparison, we are merely putting forward a hypothesis of ultimate possibilities; things will probably turn out in fact to be very different. In spite of its utopian character, the hypothesis will be worth considering, and will teach us something, for it enables us to make a preliminary survey of the possibilities brought into being by our modern inventions. It is, of course, an isolated and unilateral survey. It would be useless to pretend we can draw many conclusions from it at the human level. Yet it may be possible later to explore in greater detail and to complete our own survey with other similar ones, and so make a reasonably full inventory of the possibilities from which men will have to choose in the future and will need guidance if they are to choose well.

Let us then imagine a world in which man has succeeded in making available, at little trouble to himself, sources of energy sufficient to supply all his needs. At the same time he will have made his many industrial operations largely automatic. Such a world would, in theory, solve two of the major problems of the nineteenth and the present centuries, problems of which the brunt has been borne principally by the working classes. The first of these is that of the inadequacy of the products of industry to satisfy the requirements of all who are engaged in it. This inadequacy, it is clear, was one of the reasons for the cleavage between the principal beneficiaries of human enterprise and the proletariat. It, at least, would then disappear. The second problem is that of the inhuman character of basic industrial work, from which the worker and his opportunities of acquiring a genuine human culture have had so much to suffer. Automatic regulations would make it possible to remove this basic work from the sphere of human labour. We should not therefore inveigh against all forms of technical progress or think that moral considerations alone will resolve our difficulties. On the contrary, certain technical achievements are well able to lend their support and to succeed where moral considerations alone would exhaust themselves in fruitless efforts.

But it would be a great mistake to revive in this connection the easy, idyllic ideologies which infected the view of the future induced by the earlier advances of science and technics. The advent of a world such as we have described would not be without very grave risks for mankind. One of these has been clearly foreseen by a man who has reflected deeply on the probable effects of the new type of machinery, N. Wiener, who writes:

The modern industrial revolution is . . . bound to devalue the human brain at least in its simpler and more routine decisions. Of course, just as the skilled carpenter, the skilled mechanic, the skilled dressmaker have in some degree survived the first industrial revolution, so the skilled scientist and the skilled administrator may survive the second. However, taking the second revolution as accomplished, the average human being of mediocre attainments or less has nothing to sell which it is worth anyone's money to buy. (*Cybernetics*, published by Herman, Paris, pp. 37-38.)

Under such conditions, what kind of existence would be possible for the *average* man?

Such a question suffices to show that we cannot allow a human situation to evolve in terms of its technical factors alone. We must always bear in mind the fundamental law of man's nature which obliges him, as far as lies in his power, to adapt the events of which he is himself the cause, to the normative elements inherent in the actual state or the natural aspirations of mankind. If events should tend to evolve in the direction envisaged by our hypothesis, every care would have to be taken to preserve the economic and social roots of a large section of the inhabitants of the globe. Otherwise, we might well see the rise of social conditions far less stable than those we are at present experiencing, and perhaps leading to an inevitable and serious decrease in world population. It is quite likely that a world of material abundance in which the burden of physical toil has been eased, would prove, paradoxically enough, to be hostile to the multiplication of the human race.

Of course, this is not the only danger. It is also to be feared that the balance of power between the nations would be thrown hopelessly out of gear, if any of them, in isolation from the rest, should make great strides in the development of the new inventions. It is quite likely that, in the next phase of the process of world industrialization, a solution (if we can call it so) such as the hierarchical distinction between governing and colonial peoples would be quite impossible. It seems most unlikely that material progress will be everywhere simultaneous. It remains to be discovered how far this lack of simultaneous development will produce results which mankind can tolerate, and what types of harmonious co-operation should exist between various peoples at different stages of their evolution.

The same is true of the now possible industrialization of the processes of knowledge. There is a danger that it may be developed in a spirit similar to that of the "laissez-faire" doctrines which presided over the first industrial expansion, or on the other hand in that exactly opposite spirit which has grown up in reaction to "laissez-faire", and is found at present in the doctrines of state control. Plain "laissez-faire" might well lead to a terrible depreciation of human thought down to the level of a commercial commodity linked with the new machinery as manual labour was with the old. The managerial spirit, which has more chance of gaining the upper hand if the present situation is anything to go by, would threaten to transform this industry into one of the pillars of an administrative police organization of the world, a fate from which it is vital that mankind should be saved.

These considerations make clear that we must recognize the decisive value of a methodical use of the imagination in this sphere. We are in a different position from those who lived in the early days of machinery and industry, we can draw upon the experiences and lessons written large on the pages of the past few centuries of human history. These experiences may serve as relatively clear guides towards a considered view of the future. We should be guilty of grave negligence if we did not draw from them models for the future and from which we must attempt to gain light in making our decisions. It is scarcely possible any longer to leave mankind to work out its future unaided. We are called upon increasingly to replace the currents and crude mass pressure of vital human forces by a conscious and sound use of the intellect.

The Limits of the Mind, and Providence as a Phenomenon of historical Development

Whilst we must admit that these reflexions are highly superficial, mere vague outlines of analyses requiring to be justified and elaborated by a great effort of thought, we must once again insist on the very limited character of the information they offer. Other factors are now taking shape, whose power to influence the future is something quite new. To mention at least one example—there is the promise of great progress in the biological field. Vital phenomena are bewildering in their complexity and we have not yet any rational mastery over them. Although we seem well on the way to acquiring it, the goal may still be very distant. However, our present achievements do secure for us new powers which we shall be very tempted to combine with those given to us by the physical sciences.

What, a fortiori, will happen if we succeed in crossing the frontiers of knowledge and power which are now closed to us? Would a new world of possibilities lie open to man's endeavour just at the time when our conquest of the world of matter forced us to withdraw from it our labour and our care? Perhaps. In fact, we have little right to do more than dream our dreams and to remind ourselves that the day is perhaps not far distant when we shall have to convert our dreams into a sound system of thought.

This last example is not without its value. It reminds us that there are in man technical possibilities which his mind is powerless to delineate before they have matured organically in the course of his cultural development. At the same time that we guess at their existence, we know that we must take account of them in our study of the future and yet that it is impossible to do this in any but a negative way. All our visions of the world of the future are bound to be like the sketch plan of a play. The author begins by bringing some of the characters onto the stage, but he still has to create others, who will have to be introduced, as he well knows, although he is still ignorant of the kind of persons they will be. This situation has its repercussions on the problem of human choices, which it seems desirable to clarify by a more methodical effort from now onwards.

In the nature of things our mind is essentially limited in its power to make sound decisions. The knowledge we already have of new techniques, facts and achievements, enables us to estimate some of the future possibilities. But, at the most, we shall only have an incomplete picture and nothing guarantees in advance that this will be sufficient to enable us to hit on the choice which will prove ultimately to be the best. Our position is somewhat similar to that of a mathematician who has to determine the shortest possible distance between two points on a highly complicated surface whose peculiarities and various possible lines of communication he only knows imperfectly. It might well be that the line he puts forward as the solution is not, absolutely speaking, the shortest. It would not even be difficult to imagine a surface full of pitfalls and for which the solution which seems to stand the best chance of being correct in view of certain of the data, might eventually turn out to be thoroughly bad, when all the concrete determinants of the problem have been taken into account.

This may be the case with our conjectures as to the future of mankind. In so far as we attempt methodically to give to these the force it seems essential they should possess, we shall doubtless have to learn to be very prudent. We may perhaps be helped by the increasingly advanced theoretical researches into the value of predictions which can be based only on a partial knowledge of the data. In this way it is possible to gain some idea of the conditions which will ensure that the line of conduct we adopt in such circumstances will be dictated by *reason*. Perhaps we cannot do better than to work within this possibility of an incomplete estimate of the value of our future choices. It would already be a sign of great progress to cease to remain passive in the face of the purely reflex conditioning and haphazard choices so characteristic of some of our present decisions.

But when this has been said, we still have to remember that human history cannot possibly be reduced to a dialectic of essential factors. Though the latter play a part which it would be foolish not to recognize, they are associated on the plane of their actual existence with an enormous mass of data in constant motion; and it is impossible for us to see more in this mass than a situational fact and a contingent evolutionary process whose vagaries cut across all attempts to make human evolution more inevitable and deliberate. The present scientific and technical achievements of the human mind have come to light in the concrete context of the modern world with its highly complex geographical, anthropological and political potentialities and its unforeseen changes of direction. We can never be completely certain how this context will finally exert its influence. The case of the civilization issuing from the genius of the Greeks warns us of the immense scope of the effects which analysis is bound to show must be laid at the door of history with its crude elemental realities at work beneath the human structure of civilization and in the unpredictable spiritual factors which suddenly emerge. On the one hand the barbarians, on the other a hidden weakening in the Greek genius itself, and doubtless still more the rise of

Christianity[1] combined to interrupt—or so it would seem—the course of human development, which would have continued in quite a different way had reason alone been in control.

We may take an even more obvious example—if Archimedes had reflected on the future of mankind in terms of the knowledge his solitary genius had already begun to discover, what might not his vision of human progress have been ? After all, why, immediately after his death, should not his achievement have become a permanent possession, as had Euclid's mathematics a little before his time? However, the sword of a callous Roman soldier cut short this possibility, and we can only speculate upon it retrospectively. So to-day or to-morrow other swords may cut short the developments we anticipate. Many setbacks will delay, hold up, and distort the solid progress which would result if the course of human affairs were uniformally smooth. It is quite possible that in the world of science and technics, our time may be the prelude to serious breakdowns or to a waiting period similar to the one which separates the era of the Alexandrine scientists from that of the research workers of the Renascence. True, nothing is less certain than this eventuality; yet we are beginning to see that it is quite easy to imagine, and that is an idea which would have been impossible fifty years ago.

If it should be so, if history suddenly interrupts the continuity of those certainties which have prevailed in the West for more than three centuries, what are we to look forward to? Human labour caught in an ambush and all unknowingly set upon its own destruction? the dead weight of humanity once more triumphing over the spirit which now urges us on? Many minds would interpret the moral of history in one or other of these ways. But perhaps history prefers to reveal itself not so much in moral admonitions as by showing towards mankind, in and

[1] Renouvier's curious "Uchronie" contains some truth in this connection, fragmentary though it is and biased in it general thesis.

through its disasters, that mercy which science and technics alone are incapable of dispensing to our race. The breakdown of Greek culture made possible the assimilation of its achievements by human groups far more extensive than were those of the city states in the days of Pericles. It also led to the abandonment of those modes of thought which were fated to prevent the birth of an experimental science in the Greek mind. Finally, for Christians, there can be no doubt that it was allowed by Providence in the interests of the first propagation of the Gospel message. It may well be that mankind to-day needs a similar breakdown in our twentieth century culture and civilization. It is not for us to decide. What is certain is that no eventuality excuses us from the task of devoting all our powers to thinking out the potentialities within us, so that we may make good use of them as we prepare for the future.

CHAPTER 2

Present-Day Scientific Ideas and the Control of Human Situations

WITH the passage of time, the need for a genuinely scientific knowledge of human realities makes itself felt with increasing urgency. Economic, sociological and political phenomena although issuing from human activity, yet largely elude human control. Normally, our view of them can only be very summary and, save in exceptional cases, they are but slightly amenable to reasoned action. It even seems that the growth of civilization during the past few centuries has ended by aggravating our condition of ignorance and impotence. The free and easy empiricism of the politicians of old, and the tradition of enlightened government in the affairs of men, have become more or less out of date. At their level, reality grew in rich profusion like vegetation returning to the wild state under the ruthless pressure of life itself. Hence the astonishing fact that to-day, it is within the human race itself that we find the most numerous evidences of nature untamed by man.

Auguste Comte foresaw the advent of this new state of the human problem and already in his day dreamed of a genuinely scientific political economy with principles firmly established on the teaching of a "social" physics as coherent as was, in his view, the physics of Newton. Yet, however important the stimulus of positivism may have been in the field of the human sciences, its doctrine does not seem to have provided the means for mastering the problems raised. Even economic processes, perhaps the most accessible to methods which succeed so well in the case of physical processes, refuse to yield to any oversimplified attempt at analysis and mathematization.

The efforts which have been made have certainly not been useless. They have taught us a great deal. In particular they have made it possible to view the difficulties confronting them in the human situation, against the background of firmly established habits of scientific thought. The importance of chance in the development of processes affecting man, soon became more evident. A wholly determinist physics could only give very inadequate descriptions of "the nature of society", whose uniformity of performance, if it exists, results from circumstances in which human decisions inevitably play a part. In fact, the physics of matter, by adopting a more probabilist habit of thought, and in fields whose importance and scope are on the increase, has itself moved towards the point where its findings may be valid in the human sphere. Yet, in spite of this radical change in the climate of thought, there is still some way to go before we have a scientifically accurate description of human phenomena. Neither the kinetic theory of gases, nor the study of Brownian motion, nor the modern development of quantum mechanics, are able to give even a bare outline of the models applicable to human realities.

It is at this point that we come into contact with certain ideas, sufficiently elaborated and consistent to interest even the general public and capable, it would seem, of yielding much that is of value for the understanding of the collective human situation. These ideas appear to be grouped about two different poles, which it may be possible to pair, although up to the present, we have no practical example of any association between them. The first of these poles is "Cybernetics". The term, coined a short time ago by Wiener, has had an immediate success. The second, perhaps a little less well-known, is that of the Theory of Games, on which the studies of von Neumann and Morgenstern have recently thrown much light.

A number of books and articles on these subjects have attracted the attention of the educated public and caused it to think that science was about to grasp human phenomena in all their present complexity, and at long last open the way to the rational government of human communities. It may perhaps be useful to attempt briefly to clarify the position by indicating the positive contribution of the ideas recently brought to light—and we believe that such a contribution has been made—but without, at the same time, concealing the considerable gaps which remain between the exigencies of the subject under discussion and the resources now made available to the mind. We hope the reader will forgive us if our presentation of the essential ideas is somewhat dry, but there seems no other way to preserve their true meaning intact.

Cybernetics

This term, introduced by N. Wiener in the summer of 1947, indicates first of all a set of techniques proper to engineers specializing in the problems of telecommunication and automatic functioning. But, as Wiener's book shows[1] it is also intended to evoke the idea of a systematic analogy between this technical field and realities of an apparently totally different order. The "Cybernetician's" point of view cannot therefore be that of the technician limited to his own immediate subject; it is that of the mind always attempting to transpose to different spheres which it considers to be related, ideas it is able to acquire by the particular study of one or other of these spheres.

In point of fact, Wiener and the American cyberneticians have been much concerned with all those transferences which make it possible to relate the functioning of the living organism to the types of functioning studied by communication engineers and the designers of automatic mechanisms. Cybernetics would

[1] *Cybernetics, or Control and Communication in the Animal and the Machine.* New York, John Viley, 1948.

achieve a major triumph if it could establish a sound scientific doctrine of the similarities between the functional system of the animal—with its physiological controls, transmissions and operations effected by the nervous system—and that of the machines constructed by man. For the time being, we still seem to be at a preliminary stage of thought in this connection. Yet it already seems that some machines can help us to understand, roughly at least, certain physiological types of functioning. Conversely, at least in certain cases, the study of mechanisms in the living organism may perhaps suggest principles upon which new mechanical advances can be made.

Over and above this first class of transferences, there is the outline of a further analogy, concerned this time with the functioning of the "body politic". Cybernetics faces up to the possibilities thus revealed, although in actual fact, Wiener still shows considerable reserve in this matter. He expressly states that the application of cybernetics to human affairs is not yet really feasible.

I cannot share their feeling that the field (of human sciences) has the first claim on my attention, nor their hopefulness that sufficient progress can be registered in this direction to have an appreciable therapeutic effect in the present diseases of human society . . . the human sciences are a poor testing ground for a new mathematical technique. (*Cybernetics*, p. 34).

We are therefore warned before we begin. We must remain on the plane of ideas and conceptions which are as yet too indeterminate to be profitably utilized. We are much further away from a "social physics" capable of satisfying our scientific requirements, than we are from a science of life adequate to meet them.

In any case, the very existence of cybernetics is evidence of a new growth of awareness. Cybernetics, evolving initially in the world of the engineer, deals with facts, quite other than those with which physics has traditionally professed itself concerned. The study of the movements of bodies was the source of all classical physics. Physics, with its determinist origins, has always strictly confined its researches and formulations to the field of energy. In its view, the world is nothing but the manifold manifestation of types of energy in evolution. Complex though this manifestation undoubtedly is, yet everything in it is resolved into the flow and quantitative equilibrium of energy upon which depends the determination of observable phenomena. Concurrently with this point of view, timidly at first but then with increasing assurance as progress was made, the practice of the engineers (much more than the reflexions of the theorists) has introduced another point of view, that of what we now know as items of information. Such a point of view does not exclude the first. On the contrary it presupposes it at every step. Rather is it of a complementary nature, and can be assimilated to the traditional view somewhat as the corpuscular and wave theories are associated in quantum mechanics. In one sense, cybernetics has no less an ambition than to establish itself as a new vision of reality.

Information Theory

But what is information? The word is borrowed from the technique of communications. Men can send signals of varying character to one another through space; in the first place speech signals, then a host of others, for instance those made by waving the arms according to pre-arranged conventions, those made by opening or closing an electric circuit by means of a Morse transmitter, etc. In each case there is a signal because a certain physical reality—the sound of the voice, a luminous flux, a current—has impressed upon it by the person transmitting the signal a specific form which it is intended to convey through space to a "receptor" able to identify it. In accordance with the normal proceeding of physics, the only thing that matters to the receptor is the form to be identified. The nature of the material medium only comes up for consideration in so far as it reacts on the form by making it doubtful whether it can be accurately identified by the receptor for whom the signal is intended.

What the signal brings to the receptor is called "information". It has nothing to do with the material substratum it requires for its physical existence, but only with the form that has to be identified. If the transmission of the signal from the transmitter to the receptor does not distort the significant form, the information will be accurately received. If there is distortion, the information will be more or less corrupted. It is essential to note that the exact analysis of the conditions and the techniques of transmission allow us to go beyond the qualitative notions of the accuracy or the corruption of the information received, to the notion of a quantitative measurement of the information any given signal conveys in the course of its own evolution.

The capacity to be "the receptor of a signal" is not necessarily limited to the human consciousness. Although it would appear that conscious perception is always remotely implied, a great many appliances may be treated as receptors of signals and therefore as realities within the sphere of information and having an interest in it. Each element in a transmitting apparatus receives, conveys and elaborates information. Similarly, recording machines fix certain natural events in the form of information. Perhaps one day we shall be led to think of certain natural phenomena—such, for instance, as those of atomic physics—in terms of information, and to find that we cannot be content with the resources offered by the physics of "energy" alone.

Thus, the human mind has already entered upon a vast field, in which the advent of the information point of view is the only means of dealing adequately with the problems that now arise.

The entity "signal" has its own physics; the evolution and the interactions of the planned structures which constitute information also have their own laws. Mathematical analysis is gradually mastering these as well as those involved in the study of energy and physical quantities in the usual sense of the term.

It has been seen that it is essential to adopt this point of view not only for the theory of communications but also whenever we have to study what is known as a "regulation problem". Problems of this nature have presented themselves long since to the engineers. They are at least as old as the invention of "active" machines with their source of energy available within their own structure, and whose functioning it is desired should be geared to the performance of a specific task without human supervision. But the practical solution of these problems was found long before they were adequately studied on the theoretical plane.[1]

At this point we must go into some detail; the notion of regulation is not an easy one and it is scarcely possible to make its essential meaning clear without offering a few examples.

1. *Regulation planning*

Let S be a source of energy it is desired to employ for the performance of a complex well-defined task. Once the task is specified—for instance, the mass-production of some article or the playing of a piece of music by a machine such as the Clavichord Player constructed by Vaucanson—we have then to design a piece of apparatus D, able to effect in a coordinated manner and at the required time, the distribution and use of the energy provided by the source. This will be done, for example, by means of cams and levers adjusted in advance, which will

---

[1] Thus the ball regulator in the steam engine was already invented by James Watt circa 1770, whereas the first genuinely theoretical studies seem to have been those of J. C. Maxwell who, in 1868, published a very important paper on the automatic steering of ships.

determine the various type of work to be done by the energy entering the apparatus. Or else appropriately perforated rolls will be used, as in the case of player-pianos and many other types of apparatus. Such mechanisms function by imposing on the energy supplied in bulk by the source, a coordinated pattern of simple movements. They bring into effect mechanically the operation as planned, whilst the latter itself is determined by the result it is intended to produce.

$$S \longrightarrow \boxed{D} \longrightarrow \text{Complex result.}$$

(the regulation system is built into the actual structure of D.)

But in an apparatus so constructed, the energy is brought to the prescribed task in a rigid and uniform manner. The regulation system devised with a view to this task and laid down in advance, imposes a clearly defined pattern of behaviour on each part of the whole. The constant repetition of a complete working cycle is alone possible. In principle, therefore, chance is excluded from such a regulation system. If it should accidentally enter into the operation of the apparatus as a whole, it may jeopardize everything. For instance, if in a machine which automatically mass-produces a given product, the movement of one of the sections of the machine is not exactly what the designer intended, it is very likely that the results of this defective manufacturing process will have to be sent to the scrapheap.

This then, is one kind of mechanical regulation; it is often known as "open circuit regulation"; programmed machines, the different types of modulation of a current by a signal are all examples of this kind of regulation.

2. *Reflex-regulation*

In many cases, the type of functioning which alone is possible with such regulation systems, is not acceptable in practice, for the machine or the plant have to cope with the *unpredictable* effect of certain circumstances. A central heating apparatus is required to provide more or less heat according as the weather is more or less cold. No engineer can foresee the daily variation of temperature during any coming winter and so adjust the heating apparatus in advance accordingly. An electric plant is required to provide current for a large number of consumers. It is impossible to foresee accurately how much current these consumers will need or to impose on them a rigorously planned distribution of current. They would soon find such restrictions intolerable. The principle of prior adjustment is therefore unsuitable in such cases. If we wish the performance to be satisfactory, we have to work out an entirely different system of regulation.

Hence efforts are made to devise an apparatus having at its intake a degree of indetermination in its actual relation with the material it is to convert. For instance, in the case of ordinary machines, the energy entering the apparatus may be supplied in greater or smaller quantities. There is therefore a certain amount of latitude at the intake. Then to this basic apparatus is added a second device so designed as (1) *to record*, as they appear, the unpredictable circumstances to which the machine must respond by operating in a pre-determined manner, (2) *to determine*, on the basis of this recording, the "regulating" function, as it is called, which it is intended should modify, in the required proportions, the relation between the whole apparatus and what is fed into it at the intake, (3) *to perform* this regulating function once it is accurately determined. This second piece of mechanism therefore produces a kind of reflex coupling circuit between what happens at the "output" of the apparatus, when it encounters in its operation the unpredictable element, and what happens at the intake, when the supply coming from the "source" presents itself to be processed by the machine. It is therefore possible to give the following sketch plan of the ensemble.

Output (operation)   Intake (recording)

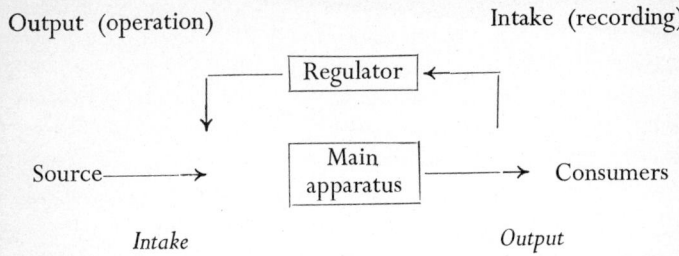

Intake	*Output*
a certain amount of latitude controlled by the regulator.	an element of chance which determined the action of the regulating system.

According to circumstances, the regulating mechanism may be very simple, e.g. the ball regulator in steam-engines, or extremely complicated. If high fidelity recording, a complex regulation pattern or more or less delicate controls at the intake are required, we shall find it necessary to have a costly, high precision apparatus. But the principle remains the same throughout the whole range of cases, from one extreme to the other.

In point of fact, we almost always consider at the output, not the unforeseen circumstance directly but the *disturbance* it is likely to produce in the running of the machine which, it is assumed, is regulated and is continuing to function on the basis of this previous regulation. When there is a disturbance, the machine does not run true, and this is usually because one of the quantities involved in its operation tends to acquire a real value other than the one it should normally have. If then, at the intake, we can arrange for another process designed to offset the irregularity, the whole ensemble can be made to run as we consider it should do, in the eventuality of a disturbance due to circumstances. Of course, there is no guarantee that this will be possible except within limits which are usually fairly narrow, and are themselves dependent on the nature of the mechanisms in action. And the success of the regulation is bound to depend too on the series of contingencies with which it has to cope. This is why the problems of mechanical construction are often so complex.

An apparatus whose functioning it has been found possible to regulate in the manner described, on the basis of the detection of the irregularities which begin to appear in it, is called a servo-mechanism. These machines are becoming extremely important to-day in all technical spheres. They also make possible the realization of leading ideas in the field of automatic regulation, for they provide examples of regulating systems capable of operating when faced with a series of *chance* events of whatever kind, whether purely physical in origin, such as the meteorological variations in temperature, or human, such as decisions left to the free choice of those who are using the machine.

Servo-mechanisms also draw attention to the functional importance of information, for we see appearing in them a kind of grading of the two operational circuits. Whereas the main body of the apparatus is designed to perform a certain task, the regulating section operates specifically at the level of information bearing upon this task and its execution. In principle at least, its borrowing from the main circuit or its discharge of energy into the latter may be non-existent. Its function is similar to that of a "Maxwell demon" and not at all like that of molecules which transfer energy. The function of regulators is to effect a transfer of *information*, not of energy.[1]

---

[1] In a sense, this transference is effected in the opposite direction from that of the transference of the forces at work in the apparatus. Hence the "reflex" (or, to use the term in vogue in English-speaking countries, *the feed-back*) pattern of the relations appearing in them. A pattern of this type is an indispensable characteristic of this kind of apparatus. At the same time, it is remarkably like a functional structure, whose integrating factor is of the psychical order, whether the function in question be merely a vital one or one which involves consciousness properly so called. It seems as though man succeeds in endowing the machine with a particle of discernment or intelligence. In the case of highly integrated systems of mechanical regulations, his success is sometimes startling.

Information and Determinism

Finally, the above facts make it possible to throw more light on the subject of information itself. Comparing the two types of regulation, we find the detailed specification of the task to be done is built firmly into the machine by its designer in the case of planned regulations, whilst with servo-mechanisms it is left to a certain extent indeterminate for the circumstances themselves to give it its precise minute to minute task. It is precisely the information brought into play in the regulating circuit of a servo-mechanism which gives their final form to the tasks the main circuit will be called upon to execute.

But information only really intervenes as and when new circumstances arise. So long as nothing out of the ordinary happens and the apparatus is functioning properly, the machine, like any other, follows a determined and unvarying pattern of behaviour, and the regulating section of the plant does not intervene. All the information is, so to speak, fixed and static in the very structure of the main body of the machine, just as it is in the planned regulation incorporated into the mechanism of open circuit systems.

In fact, therefore, information only appears as an entity to be considered for its own sake, when, in any complex system of realities, there occur deviations from the determinist evolution of the system. In a complex system evolving on strictly determinist lines, the structural determination of its reality is summed up completely in the description of its initial conditions, and the passage of time merely transforms it within the terms of reference of these conditions. From any given state of the system, any other state at any other time, could be inferred. When, on the contrary, events outside this determinist evolution, from whatever source, begin to exist within an evolving complex system, there is new information and, as such, it may influence the whole subsequent evolution. Information then begins to play, in the course of the process, a particular and essential part, which obliges us to consider it for its own sake.

On the whole, the determinist evolution of a complex system may be considered to determine a kind of physical null point of information, somewhat similar to a zero potential. It is only when chance events appear that there is any question of information playing a part at the physical level. We see why classical physics never looked at things from the standpoint of information. Its determinist doctrine quite simply prevented information from coming into the picture at all. We also see why information techniques lead to a concept of evolution and of time so different from that envisaged by Newtonian physics.[1]

For the physicist, however, information never appears except against a determinist background. This is why he will attempt to construct models of it, based on representations as like as may be to those valid for events in a determinist situation. One of these representations is that of a physical quantity, which, instead of acquiring with the passage of time a series of values all of which are fixed by a determinist evolution, acquires some at least of these values by chance. That is to say, at certain times these values appear to have been drawn by lot from a whole host of possibilities, each having its own degree of probability. The result of each of these chance determinations then constitutes an element of particular and significant information bearing on the evolution of the quantity in question considered in a time sequence. English-speaking engineers are accustomed to calling the time sequences of these determinations "time-series". In France, the term "chronique" is preferred to describe these unpredictable variations in physical quantity.[2] Except at its

---

[1] This is one of the reasons why Wiener devotes the first chapter of his "Cybernetics" to a comparison between the ideas implicit in the Newtonian and Bergsonian views of time. The Newtonian view of physics excludes any essential renewal of 'the face of things' in the course of time. Such a renewal is demanded by the Bergsonian concept of concrete duration.

[2] We owe to G. Th. Guilbaud the term "chronique" as characterizing these descriptions of items of information which enter one after the other into the picture.

origin, the "chronique" of determinism has no content at all.

A simple servo-mechanism merely brings into being a machine able, to some extent at least, to respond coherently and permanently to a chance event represented by the non-determined variation of a single physical quantity. This response capacity depends essentially on the successive readings in the time-series of the quantity, readings connected with various general *a priori* conjectures as to the probable course of the time-series itself. Thus the functioning of a servo-mechanism is seen as a kind of dialogue in time with chance. There is then nothing to stop us from thinking out combinations and gradings of various servo-mechanisms as complex as we like. This, technics does not hesitate to do, but there is no need to labour the point here.

Yet chance may quite well originate in human activity. As far as engineers are concerned, this is most often the case. Man stands on the horizon both at the intake and at the output ends of the machines and plant which serve his needs. He is present, especially through the unforeseeable demands he may make and which continually create new situations in the complex structure of the realities in evolution. Cybernetics *is*, therefore, already a science of mankind and of human realities to the extent that man's presence is linked to the chance element in the various time-series of reality, to the extent also that the study of reflex regulations is the study of the adaptation of mechanisms to the changes in the time-series. True, it is a science in which, by comparison with the part played by physics, the human element in the subject studied is more restricted than in any other. But it is a science that marks the first step along a path upon which we may hope to meet the problems of economics and mass psychology, though at a very much later stage.

The Theory of Games

Mathematicians have long been interested in the way human

beings play their games. Pascal saw in it the first elements of a theory of probabilities. Many scientists then examined the structure of games and analysed the various possibilities that arise in the course of play. But the idea of studying a game as the formulation of a series of human decisions and of considering the general relations of these series of decisions to the result of the game, is relatively recent. This study after being sketched out over the past few decades has now taken shape in an important book by J. von Neumann and O. Morgenstern[1]. The importance of this work consists not only in the fact that it is centred on the human element in games, but also in the fact that it outlines a relatively clear connection with the problems of economic science. For the playing of a game has its *economic* side. There are stakes and the players have to make sure that they will win as much as they can or reduce their losses to a minimum. It is to this aspect of play that we wish to draw attention for the moment. In so doing, we place ourselves at a rather different standpoint from that normally taken by psychology which loosely connects the economic with the other interests presented by games.

In any case, for each player, a particular game of a given type—chess, poker, etc.—consists of a series of moves or hands played in rotation according to certain rules. It is assumed that there is no cheating. The different partners, by their respective moves or play, cause a certain situation to evolve, which is determined by the game itself. It begins with an initial situation and ends with another that leads to the settlement of accounts between the players. This evolution is discontinuous. The moves or hands which develop it are a discrete series. It is problematical. Each move or hand is played by a player who is ordinarily faced with a number of possibilities. His choice is determined either by a purely material chance—the dealing of the cards, the throwing of

[1] *Theory of Games and Economic Behaviour*, University Press, Princeton, 1944.

PRESENT-DAY SCIENTIFIC IDEAS 41

the dice, etc.—or by a deliberate decision—chess, playing to win the trick at cards, etc.

In ordinary games the possibilities at each move are finite in number. Further, there are rules which, directly or indirectly, ensure the finite character of the series of moves of which the game is composed. The number of all possible particular games is therefore itself finite.[1]

Let us suppose a player thinks beforehand about the game he proposes to play with the intention of winning as much as possible. In theory at least, he can imagine the complete set of situations in which any player may find himself in the course of any particular game.[2] Similarly, he can work out for each situation the complete series of possibilities it offers. He can then construct, in relation to each of the partners in the game (his opponents as well as himself) the complete schedule of the series of decisions (finite in number) which may possibly be made by a player in a particular game. These series are called "strategies".[3] By examining the overall picture of his own strategic possibilities, and by comparing these with those of his partners, the player can draw certain

[1] This discrete and finite character is one of the points at which the progress of games differs most from what we normally know by intuition of natural processes, which appear to be unlimited and continuous.

[2] In the original French, the game as such, i.e. chess, bridge, etc., is indicated by the word "jeu", whereas the word "partie" is used for one game of chess or bridge as distinct from another. In the case of football, etc., English has the word "match". In translating when the reference, as in the text, is to games such as chess and cards, I have rendered the word "partie" by "particular game"—.*Translator's note.*

[3] The details of such sequences may be set out as follows—Strategy for X; —If at the moment of his first move X is in the situation A1, then he plays a1; if in A2, then he plays a2, etc. If at his second move X is in situation B1, then he plays b1, etc. For any given player a strategy may remain the same for many different particular games, for it constitutes only one course of action, in circumstances over which the partners exercise control. But it goes without saying that when all the partners have fixed, each for himself, the strategy they intend to adopt, the particular game can only be played in one way. Every individual game is therefore equivalent to a choice, made independently but simultaneously by each of the partners, of a strategy proper to himself which will be linked to or opposed to the other strategies used in the course of play.

D

conclusions about the advantages or disadvantages in adopting this or that strategy, it being assumed that the other partners are capable of thinking things out as thoroughly from their point of view.

The theory reveals the following facts. In the first place, in games where there are two players, when the situations arising for both of them in the course of play allow of a knowledge of all the elements in the moves to be made, then there exists, in the case of one of the players, one strategy at least, which will infallibly cause him either to win or draw, whatever strategy may be used against him by his opponent. On the latter hypothesis, the opponent too, may always draw. This is the case with chess.[1] Where the situations arising leave the players in ignorance of some of the factors involved in the hand to be played—as is the case normally with card games—there is usually no strategy that is decisive, irrespective of the opponent's play. But, in the course of a series of particular games, there are ways in which each player may vary his strategies with a maximum mathematical expectation of winning.

If, however, the number of players is more than two, there exists normally no strategy or system of strategical variations capable of giving the individual player a maximum mathematical expectation of winning. Everything, in fact, depends on the character of the combined strategies brought to bear by the other players taken as a whole. Now this combination of strategies is the result of free interplay evolving according to chance, unless it has been intentionally agreed upon before the game by the players who bring it into operation. Finally, as all the players,

---

[1] The theorem thus established, and which is valid in the case of chess, does not in any sense mean that we know *ipso facto* whether chess if perfectly played by both partners ends or not in a draw, nor, if it does not, which player has the advantage. Still less do we know what strategy is the one which will ensure that he will always win. In the case of chess, all this still remains unknown because of the enormous (though finite) mass of possibilities which would have to be examined if complete answers are to be given to these questions.

each on his own account, find themselves in a similar position, it will be obvious that certain players may associate to ensure that collectively they have an expectation of winning greater than the sum of the expectations each member could be sure of individually. The play will then tend of itself to reveal the arrangements which have been made beforehand by the players. These arrangements will aim at constituting groups to coordinate most effectively the decisions of the individuals.

It is precisely the possible points of equilibrium in such circumstances that the Theory of Games principally studies. This study might be thought to be relatively easy. In fact, it soon becomes clear that it is extremely complex. So far, only the case of three players has been completely worked out.

At first sight, it will doubtless be asked what is the point of these very abstract considerations which can, in any case, only have quite rare applications, even in the actual playing of games. Their complexity is already so great that it is impossible, with the means ordinarily at our disposal, to make a complete study of their strategic possibilities. The importance of the Theory of Games lies, however, in the fact that it allows us, for the first time, to see clearly the connection between a certain economic end—the money to be won—and a pattern of human actions coordinated in terms of other human activities, but equally in terms of certain material conditions. Thus the game is a kind of very simplified economy, taking shape in a finite and discrete context. For the moment, it is the only approximation to economic realities which we can consider to be scientifically well defined on the theoretical plane. It is of course a very rudimentary approximation. Yet it is enough to constitute a step forward, and a very characteristic one, in the science of human processes.[1]

[1]For the significance of the Theory of Games in the field of economic science, see the important article by G. Guilbaud in *Economie appliquée*, vol. II, number 2, April-June, 1949 (Presses universitaires de France).

A few possible Points of Contact between Cybernetics and the Theory of Games

If some of the concepts elaborated independently by the Theory of Games are considered from the point of view of Cybernetics, their implications seem easier to grasp. The series of moves to be made by a player in the course of a particular game is in many respects like the series of chance events which we find to be the determining factor in the problem of feed-back regulation. Similarly, the regulation mechanism which, when confronted with each of these events, elaborates the response appropriate to the machine, is not at all unlike a strategy in certain of its characteristics.

The chief weakness of this analogy, it is true, is that it attempts to compare a discrete and finite case—that of games—with one which is normally continuous and infinite—that of the regulation processes studied by Cybernetics. Nevertheless the analogy may be completed if we take note of certain other features. The opposing interests characteristic of games, may be found even in regulation processes. Thus in the case of the aeroplane attacked by an automatically controlled battery, the interest of the plane is, in fact, diametrically opposed to that of the battery, and this fact can be mathematically represented in much the same terms as those formulated by the Theory of Games for the opposition of interests between players. The fact that it is thus possible to transfer into the sphere of Cybernetics an essential element of the Theory of Games, confirms the analogy and may itself have a certain heuristic value.

In particular it throws light on the question of the possible relations between a series of chance events (observed from outside and assumed to be the product of a specific activity) and the master plan directing this activity of which the events are the manifestation. Indeed, the actual play of the player during the game is one thing, his strategy another. The pilot of the aircraft in the line of fire observes the bursting of a number of shells fired at him, but he does not fail also to assume that the enemy is using a certain method in the pursuit of his target. He may even have some preliminary idea of what this method is. In any case, his observations can give him some information on this point. Can he, on the basis of such information, plot out his own movements in the danger zone in such a way that he may more easily escape? We have here a problem very similar to the one which would arise in the Theory of Games, were we to attempt to elaborate an optimum strategy where something is known of the opponent's usual style of play.

Thus we have an outline translation into scientific terms—on a certain plane at least—of the relation existing between the *conduct* of the individual, the externalized, physically observable part of his behaviour, and the system of inner principles governing this conduct, that part of his behaviour beyond the immediate grasp of physical observation, but which the mind can reconstitute to a certain extent by observing behaviour. The Theory of Games with its notion of strategy provides one description of these principles, and Cybernetics another with its notion of regulation. Engineers, who instinctively enter into a relation of partnership with their raw materials, are always, in their own way, establishing a similar outlook on the nature of the cosmos itself.

In constructing their machines, they continually bring to bear not only their observations of the way Nature behaves, but also hypotheses which instinctively suggest themselves concerning the principles underlying natural behaviour. The first of these technical hypotheses concerning Nature's strategy is that of the determinist series of processes which follow once the initial conditions have been laid down. Ultimately, when the mind is obliged to reckon with something other than this determinist series, it instinctively forms hypotheses concerning the working of those chance determinants whose existence is attested by the natural processes themselves. Almost all servo-mechanical regulation systems are constructed on the supposition that chance data are involved and that they occur in "stationary" series.[1] We may say then, that the engineer thinks of nature, in the first place as being as determinist as possible, in the second, as being as "stationary" as possible, and thirdly . . . but that remains to be seen. Thus human industry is revealed as containing a whole unconscious philosophy antecedent to any formulation at the speculative level.

Towards a Mathematization of Human Situations. Possibilities and Obstacles

These considerations seem irrelevant in human cases. But, in fact, this is by no means so. We always attempt to acquire scientific knowledge of human processes by trying to discover points of view from which they may be assimilated to those natural processes we can understand. It was scarcely possible for determinist physics to provide us with means to deal with processes where there is a specific human intervention, for human initiative always introduces the element of chance. On the other hand, indeterminist physics, whose development is ever on the increase, does open the way for a few elementary discussions. There seem, in fact, to be many cases where human behaviour, resulting from a scarcely conscious exercise of freedom, entirely conditioned by nature, produces little beyond a more or less

[1] A chance series of events is called stationary when the law of probability in regard to the occurrence of the events at a given moment does not vary with the passage of time. It is not always the same events which actually take place—for instance, the value of a certain quantity will not be constant with the passage of time. But whatever the actual value assumed at any given moment, the probability of this value remains constant all the time, fixed as it is, by a law governing the distribution of the probability of values, a law that remains unchanged throughout the period of duration. Many cases of natural and human events satisfy this condition.

stationary series of events, which we may hope will come increasingly within the range of scientific knowledge.[1]

In any case, Cybernetics and the Theory of Games, each in its own way, lead the mind to propound in very general terms certain problems concerning networks of relations. The functional character of these relations can be defined and studied apart from the concrete cases which furnish us with the first examples of their interplay. We have here the beginnings of a new algebra. We have only aninkling of its difficulties and also of its power. Its models and therefore its applications may be found simultaneously in the fields of natural realities, mechanical apparatus, biological structures, psychological complexes and human processes. It is certain that the scientific mind is beginning to learn a new language, although for the moment, we are only able to stammer out its first few words. We must summon the help not only of Cybernetics, the Theory of Games and abstract algebra, but also of mathematical logic, unprofitable though it is often said to be. It is not by chance alone that some of the English-speaking "cyberneticians" are well aware of its views and problems, and that a paper, written jointly by several of them, bears the title 'Logical Calculations of the Ideas immanent in Nervous Activity''. (See Wiener's *Cybernetics*, *p.21*)

Finally, we note that the problems of this new scientific language are coming to the fore at the very moment when technics is actually providing men with the first tools needed for the work it entails. The concrete resources available for the activity of brain and mind are inadequate to cope with the immense complexity of the simplest problems that have to be faced. We have only to imagine, to take one example, what would be involved in an exhaustive study of the possible strategies

[1] But note the reservations expressed later. Human affairs are often fairly "stationary" on a short and unreflecting view, they are rarely so on a long view, and the advent of a greater degree of awareness may entirely alter the whole situation.

in chess or bridge. We very soon reach possibilities whose number is greater than that of the atoms in our universe. But matters with which the human intellect can in practice deal only within very confined limits, may be more extensively explored by calculating machines. At this level, we shall no longer think and talk unaided, our thought will be extended by means of a whole host of prefabricated "faculties", which it is now both necessary and possible for us to manufacture. Many of the topics now investigated by human sciences are of this type. They are beyond the reach of our unaided intellect, but the new tools now placed at the service of our reason are able to take us to them.

Developing ideas and mechanical inventions thus cooperate with one another; scientific facts we have long known combine to form entirely new structures. Symbolical logic, algebra in its most abstract forms, numerous biological and psychological researches, the resources proper to each of these disciplines are all mobilized on a new front by the new aims of the science of mankind. Now that the alchemy of matter appears almost fully to have attained its original goal, the mind is surely called to the higher study of the alchemy of history, which is scarcely yet within our reach. Comte's project now seems about to be realized, and the time may not be very far distant when, as Plato long ago desired, the ideal world of mathematical accuracy may become the authentic model for politics and the source of peace within society.

Yet we must not imagine we have already reached the end of our journey. It is only now that we are setting out upon it. Once more, we must note the sceptical attitude of the leaders in the field of Cybernetics in regard to the immediate application of their ideas to the sphere of human realities. It is perhaps possible to throw some light on the reasons why we think we shall have to grope our way forward for a long time to come before the possibilities we now dimly descry begin to be of real use to us. We have seen that in fact human considerations are beginning to intervene in the processes studied and mastered by Cybernetics. Chance variations in the requirements of a group of consumers are the human term in many problems of regulation. But we observe that the human element intervenes in such problems to a very small extent and at one point only. All the rest is in the mechanical order and physically determined, to such an extent that it requires an effort *not* to think of the whole structure as a purely mechanical system. Now the commonest human processes mostly involve human factors on a far greater scale. Instead of being purely mechanical like industrial machinery, economic, social, political and cultural mechanisms ordinarily include a whole mass of human constituents. The mutual relations of the latter are very different from those existing between the parts of purely mechanical appliances, or even of those which involve a human element. Although we know how material machinery is constructed, we really know almost nothing about social "machinery", large numbers of whose organs are simply networks of human relations. Cybernetics in its present state is very inadequate in this sphere, and we have but little hope of seeing it master at all rapidly even the bare essentials of the problem.

Secondly, even in the most simple case, viz., that of the primary relation between the human element and an entirely physico-mechanical system, we again meet the essential difficulty pointed out by Wiener. Although we are able for a series of physical events to define and realize an adequate uniformity in the conditions under which they occur, we are quite unable to do anything like this in the human sphere. To take an example, the permanence of thermodynamic phenomena is easy to conceive. We see nothing outrageous in the idea that in the far distant future, there will be laboratories capable of carrying out the same experiments as our own, and we believe that their research workers would produce series of events similar to those we produce to-day. On the other hand, we cannot conceive of a similar possibility when the material studied is nothing but a human datum. Five thousand years ago, human phenomena were certainly not what they are to-day, for the circumstances under which they were produced were themselves human and have been carried away by the ebb and flow of man's evolution.

In other words, although physics instinctively thinks of its laws as absolutely permanent, of its methods of scientific definition as universal, and so considers its subject matter as in a sense outside time, yet it is obvious that the science of human phenomena must abandon this idea of permanence. The nature of human phenomena, the laws of their whole universe, change with the passage of time. The time-series of a human process does not long retain its analogy with its physical model, as is shown by human statistics covering a period of time. In order to draw valid conclusions from time-series, physics requires the latter to be capable of preserving the same significance for a *long period of time*. Thus there arise difficulties from which we cannot yet escape, since they are so new in the field of our scientific apperception.

Finally, when we inquire into this variability of human affairs, we soon notice that it depends, partly at least, on a source so unique in comparison with physical realities, that we find it very difficult to subject it, from any angle, to a theoretical study and a scientific symbolization. Variation in human affairs is not indeed merely due to a more or less continuous transformation of the general circumstances in which human acts take place; it is equally due to the entry into the picture of the factor of "increased awareness", and to the individual and collective reactions of the human beings who reach this state of increased awareness. For man reflects upon himself at the same time as he develops by a natural, spontaneous process. This continual assumption of evolution into the sphere of reflexion, together with man's power of transposing the realities of his existence from one sphere to another, are facts of which our synthetic and analytical faculties have the greatest difficulty in constructing clear images, even of the most general and inadequate kind. If we remember that we are still without a *logic* of reflexion, it will be realized that we are still very far from providing it with a genuinely scientific *physics*. Dialectics, in the modern sense of the term, has certainly foreseen the problem, but its utterances upon the subject are still halting and infantile.

All these remarks help us, so we hope, to realize the distance separating our present speculations from an adequate scientific grasp of human affairs by the human mind. Without in any way wishing to discourage the spirit of invention, which is now discovering such a stupendous career for itself in the field of human realities, we nevertheless hope that what we have written will help to calm the fears of those who, seeing mankind still largely bound by the chains of evil, think anxiously of what the future may hold in store. If the future should serve the powers of evil, the resources of government based on genuine scientific knowledge might certainly lead to disasters beyond the reach of our imagination. But these resources have hardly begun to exist. There is time for us to think, without giving way to those gruesome fantasies with which many to-day like to terrify themselves and those who listen to them. We have time to think. We are in duty bound to think.

CHAPTER 3

NEW TECHNIQUES AND THE FUTURE OF MANKIND

AFTER the second World War we are beginning to have some idea of what the future holds in store, at least in some of its aspects. Not that the latter appear in the form of certainties upon which the nations may rely if they are to determine unequivocally what aspirations are legitimate and what undertakings are reasonable. No nation can say 'Today I shall do this, tomorrow I shall set to work on such and such a scheme,' without taking into account possible situational changes and the sudden violent upheavals of history. Too many things in this world have been thrown out of gear, too many uncontrolled forces have been unleashed and have so far failed to find their equilibrium, and no nation can develop in security the resources given to it by God, by nature and by its own history. In this respect, our time is one of ominous uncertainty.

Yet, over and above national differences, at the somewhat higher level of the great facts of our total human situation, certain conditions are beginning to establish themselves. These conditions are now clear enough to make it advisable for us to consider them. They do not provide a solution to our problems, but they do enlighten us as to the way these problems present themselves, whilst leaving us responsible for the ideas and the courses of action upon which depends, for better or for worse, the destiny of the modern world. The following remarks are only a small contribution to the efforts this task demands of us, and they do not claim to do more than give a bare outline of the elements of one of these conditions and of the problems it raises.

A civilization does not consist of mere technical development. Many are so convinced of this that, among all man's endowments, they look on his technical assets as the least noble and the most unimportant of his possessions. They would almost go so far as to hold the same view of technics—bound up too closely with work in the purely material order and with the pursuit of economic gain—as the Greek mind held in regard to servile work and the compulsion it entailed. But history teaches us that there is reason to modify this verdict and to adopt towards technics a less disparaging attitude than that of the ancient philosophers. Of itself, technical development is not civilization. Yet there are profound links between those human activities which are devoted to the exploitation of the material world (if we take them as a whole), and the development of the higher values of the spirit. It would, of course, be absurd, to think there is a direct and necessary correspondence between them. In many cases, an immediate and exaggerated concern with material well-being and technical progress can stifle all else and lead to the decline of true civilization. Yet in spite of the ever-present possibility of such degeneration, in spite also of its too frequent occurrence, it remains largely true that the two movements go hand in hand. The history of mankind, as we are beginning to see it to-day, presents us with the overall picture of a simultaneous advance both on the plane of technical achievement and on that of progress towards spiritual maturity.

This does not mean that the level of technical achievement to-day should be, as between nations, a measure of the spiritual capital each possesses. This, too, would be absurd. Our present considerations are concerned only with humanity as a whole, not with a comparison between the nations of which it is composed. Nevertheless, it remains true that, at the level of humanity as a whole, the growth of our technical powers calls so irresistibly for a spiritual advance that hitherto, through a multitude of troubles, failures, crimes across the long centuries, man has always if slowly answered this call. What we know of the first great technical achievements of mankind in the neolithic period—agriculture, specialized crafts, the first organization of complex human societies—is itself sufficient to make us guess how immense was the enlargement of man's spiritual horizons which went with this great step forward on the most material plane of his life.

All other things being equal, we cannot fail to recognize the strong upward movement of the spirit which, in the human race as it has been civilized in modern times, brings its influence to bear simultaneously with the powerful growth of technical resources that began in the European middle ages and has continued with increasing intensity for the past three centuries. Even our scathing criticisms of a world in the grip of technics, even the anguish of mind so many of our writers reveal in their novels describing the future that awaits us, are only the outward and vigorous sign of the spiritual need awakened in the soul of modern man by the technical triumphs of our times. If we realize so clearly that the things which make man truly great may fall into contempt and decay, it is because we do not wish this contempt to prevail, it is because we refuse with all our being to accept this decay.

Nevertheless, the Christian knows that there is a definite limit to this deep-seated sense of a positive connexion between technical progress and man's spiritual growth. By bringing into the world the values of eternal life, Christ—and with him all that derives from the Gospel; the spread of the Faith, the works of charity, the life of the Church—gives birth in the heart of man to a spiritual element which is quite beyond the scope of any law of dependence upon man's material progress. Divine grace may transform any poor wretch into a son of God radiant with a glory far surpassing that of those most gifted in the natural order ; by the same token it matters little to Christianity whether

NEW TECHNIQUES AND FUTURE OF MANKIND 55

or not its true inner life conforms to the laws of human progress.

Yet, while reminding man of the transcendence and gratuitousness of the divine gifts, Christianity as a force in history, far from disturbing the natural order of human life, tends, so it would seem, to confirm it and even to give it a solid basis which it might not have if left to itself. Christ was neither Greek nor Roman, but he willed to be born in a human *milieu* from which his message could easily reach that section of mankind which at that time had made the greatest progress in the natural order. The ancient civilization lay partly in ruins, yet it was renewed and extended by the barbarian invasions until it covered the whole of Europe; and Christianity, once it had entered into possession, slowly prepared the European mind to assert with new force the manifold powers of reason. It was no mere chance that the modern conquest of nature had its beginnings in Christian Europe. Though Christianity infinitely transcends the sphere of man's earthly existence, yet it is fitting that it should thus assist man to derive all the benefit he can from created things.

But from now onward, such generalizations are no longer enough. We must note once more that mankind has never advanced along the path of technical progress as one body. Whenever a great step forward is taken, a group breaks away from the mass of humanity in travail, a group to which is entrusted the essential task of conquering new territories. This human group achieves its triumphs alone and fairly rapidly, on its own account. The rest of the world only shares in its success later by slowly following the example of the pioneers. The great neolithic civilization which was the prelude to our own era arose in Chaldea and Lower Egypt, and later spread throughout the Mediterranean world and to other regions of the globe. Among the nations of this Mediterranean world, Greece and Rome were subsequently the only ones who made any further advance. Still later, Europe again moved forward alone, and so inaugurated the present state of civilization. In this matter of human progress there is never any uniformity among the peoples of the earth.

It follows that, in the very nature of things, there comes a time when the technical progress which sustains a civilization in its upward movement, brings to the human group which has achieved it, the need for new spheres of action and at the same time incomparable resources of power. Here lies the origin of great imperial destinies. Technical advances inevitably make man a conqueror. A people which lags behind in this field is condemned to be dominated by others. Assyria, Egypt, Rome, Europe from the end of the Middle Ages down to our own times, exemplify this law in human affairs.

Hence, we should be foolish not to heed the lessons contained for our instruction in the destiny of Europe, for they are still very much to the point. Our decisive technical superiority from the thirteenth century onward has made us free of the whole world and given us the means whereby we have imposed our system on all the peoples of the earth. It has been our ambition to bring the Gospel to them and in this we have partly succeeded. But together with the Gospel, we have brought ourselves as conquerors and colonizers. Together with the often harsh realities of our conquest and colonization, we have instilled something of our own civilization. To-day, we see it implanted everywhere, at least in the most material aspects of its achievement, in particular, technics, industry, our economic system and the way of life it involves.

We have conquered the world. The European nations have combined to assume responsibility for the imperialist policy resulting from our material triumphs. To-day we know that this era of specifically European expansion is past. Already we are in a position to attempt to draw up a balance sheet of our undertakings in a more detached frame of mind. We have abolished the geographical boundaries which, until only a few centuries ago, inevitably shut in civilizations upon themselves. We have imposed certain common material standards on the whole world; our success has varied in different areas, but has always apparently been sufficient to ensure that the effects of our influence should be lasting. The future will build upon these foundations long after all that still remains of the domination of the European nations has disappeared. Herein lies the greatness of Europe, and her imperishable achievement.

Yet, in spite of this greatness, it seems that any European conscience worthy of the name, cannot but suffer from a sense of shame and remorse as it contemplates the work we have done. We have done what we could and we have done it as well as we could, weak and sinful men that we are, in spite of the Cross of Christ. Surely too much should not have been expected of us. But to-day, we can see more clearly the weaknesses in our achievement. We have imposed upon the world a certain common material standard of life, an economic system, a political system, an art of war, but we ought to have united the highest spiritual values we have ourselves inherited, with those less exalted perhaps but by no means unworthy, which form part of the patrimony of those peoples with whom the irresistible force of our expansion has brought us into contact. This we have failed to do. We have destroyed much, we have alienated the hearts of many. Though we have exercised our spiritual prerogatives all over the earth, we have not listened perhaps, in the midst of our successes, to a sound God hears above all the clamour of our world—the mute cry of suffering that rises to him from the souls of the oppressed. We have done great things, but we have too often failed to do them in a spirit of love.

No doubt this is the law of conquest and the natural play of the forces that determine the rise of empires. But we must take note of the human losses resulting from what we still call the inexorable course of history. At first sight it might be thought that mankind consists of groups very differently situated as regards the power to renew their culture and vital spirit. At a given period, each group seems to have separated from the more active sector and to have decided to build its own life principally on the basis of what has been already achieved; but by so doing, it denies itself the possession of the means to progress. Further progress will then be the work of others, and only its results and effects will eventually leave their mark—and that in a purely external manner—on a way of life established on such a foundation. The most primitive peoples have never advanced beyond a certain point. Other peoples have gone further. Others again are in the van of progress. There seems therefore to be a kind of hierarchy.

To judge by the evidence of history, this hierarchy appears to be very rigid and inflexible. The urge to progress and conquest does not, so it would seem, return to those human groups which have allowed themselves to be outdistanced—whether deliberately or unconsciously matters but little. Their subsequent share in the results of human progress remains something entirely alien to them. They submit to it, they benefit by it, but they do not make it their own, they do not develop it further. At the most, they treat it in many cases as a familiar garment, and their soul remains unaffected by it. If the soul is affected, it unfortunately so often happens that it is destroyed and its place is not taken by the spirit of the peoples to whose efforts the progress is due.

Is this then an inevitable condition of human life ? This is a difficult question to answer. But perhaps the apparently irreversible direction in the destiny of human collectivities which separates them one by one from the rest, arises above all from the violence of the impact of the most advanced group upon those whose forward march is slower. It is probably unjust and untrue to allege that there is an inner failure of human powers in those who are evidently in an inferior position.

The dominant sector of mankind in the fullness of its power thinks it is enough to dominate in order to bring to all the civilization by which it itself lives. But in that case, it brings only its power, not its soul. Far from opening the way to a higher spiritual relationship, far from initiating others into the exploits of its own genius, it condemns to an inferior status the very people its power oppresses. What the laziness and backwardness of these peoples would not be able completely to obliterate, may well be ruined beyond repair by the violence of a conqueror. If we think of the last few European centuries in the light of this fact, it will be easy to convince ourselves that the pride of life has unconsciously crept into our movements of expansion. We have not loved enough those peoples to whom the material and technical progress of our civilization has forced us to go, and in them, we have suppressed, perhaps for centuries to come, the possibility of their sharing, if not in the externals of our way of life which we have imposed upon them, at least in that which is surely the best in ourselves.

At this precise moment when we whom the fullness of European civilization has brought to maturity, are beginning to make our examination of conscience, we find there is far more for us to do than indulge in sterile regrets. In fact, we are about to live through—and this time consciously—a new cleavage in our own human group on the plane of technical progress. The problem facing us is whether, when this cleavage takes place, the old blind historic forces are once again to enter into play, or whether on the contrary, we shall have sufficient strength of mind to alter the course of history. We are men of ancient European stock and we are perhaps ill-prepared to appreciate the importance of certain recent technical facts. It is impossible here to make a complete analysis of the present situation, but a few simple remarks will be sufficient to give a direction to our thought.

Two great series of scientific and technical events cover the most significant progress achieved by modern man. Mankind has now reached a stage when the possibilities regarding the use of nuclear energy are already considerable. We are also quite rapidly becoming aware of new resources now available to knowledge and for the rational control of complex processes ranging from those of biology to those of human sociology. On the one hand, the atomic bomb and on the other, the very recent construction of huge electronic calculating machines, are the most spectacular evidences of the possessions the human mind is now in the act of acquiring.

The most spectacular evidences, but not the most important. Hitherto the conquest of nuclear energy has been considered important principally as providing a new type of military potential. Yet, behind the weapon, lies the possibility—doubtless more difficult to bring into effect but fraught with far greater ultimate consequences—of a whole new human industry. The next half century should see its achievements in considerable numbers. Already many efforts are being made with a view to developing the peaceful, industrial uses of nuclear energy. There is reason to think that the latter will succeed, and fairly rapidly, in revolutionizing many problems of production and economy.

In the same way, the construction of great electronic machines and more generally, the practical applications of what is known now as Cybernetics, are facts sufficiently outstanding to attract the attention of the public. Yet it seems that we should attach still more importance to the general direction of the research work which controls these applications. What is now envisaged is (a) the construction of powerful " information machines " dealing with extremely complex realities : (b) the assembling of rationalized machinery capable of controlling processes which from now onward will be very different from those of pure mechanics, since these processes may, should the occasion arise, include the play of human activity in all its forms. A kind of industry of knowledge and its applications is thus adumbrated. It is quite simply intended that the powers of the human brain should be extended by means of machinery and, if necessary, by genuine factories whose task will consist in elaborating scientifically decisions to which thought is powerless to give a rational form directly. Here again, mankind will soon become aware, through its many practical results, of the hidden power in the instrument which technics is now attempting to forge.

Now it is also a fact that, in the field of these advances which are very probably essential for the future of mankind, the different peoples of the European community now occupy very different positions. Only a small number of them are in possession of nuclear energy, and then in varying degrees. The gap between American achievements and the French atomic pile is enormous. Although the situation is not so clear concerning research into the techniques of information and control, yet it is by no means certain that all the European peoples have the same awareness regarding what can be done in this sphere, or the same willingness to undertake it. Here again, the American genius seems to be in a dominating position and through the sheer material strength of a more childlike audacity coupled with greater resources, to take up an attitude towards these things which fails to interest many other countries because they are in a sense more inwardly mature.

Further, there is little chance that a mere intellectual interest in these things would suffice to reduce the gap which tends, as we have said, to appear between the nations of the old and the new European civilization. Rivalry would only be possible if there were some sort of equality in the matter of material resources, and perhaps too a certain definite determination to co-ordinate human efforts. These requirements appear to be outside the range of European peoples, who are still roughly equal on the scientific, technical and industrial planes. A difference in the material situation and a psychological climate both seem to play the decisive role of factors of division. To take only one example, the United States are able to make of scientific research and the systematic study of its practical applications a genuine branch of industry, whereas the old European civilization still cannot see any possibility other than the noble labour of the individual scientist or the isolated laboratory. If, for instance, we French were willing to attempt these new ways of approaching problems, our efforts would very soon be restricted by material obstacles, and our achievements would be on a scale distinctly inferior to that which is possible elsewhere.

Let us make no mistake about it; within the community of European culture, these facts may determine breaks in the level of civilization as important as that which occurred from the thirteenth century onward between Christian Europe and the Islamic world, when the latter was distinctly outdistanced by the former, although two centuries earlier, both seemed to be on a roughly equal footing. These facts then may eventually determine the rise, even among ourselves, of new imperialisms, developing under new forms and threatening to reduce a considerable section of what still constitutes a single community, purely and simply to the status of subject colonies. It may, after all, be worth our while to dwell upon the possibility that the course of history could make of Western Europe a region of backward peoples under the control of a sovereign but alien power and of men belonging to a culture practically inaccessible to Europeans. The mere phenomena of technical progress and their historical consequences may well lead eventually to such a state of affairs. It is impossible to attempt to defend ourselves against it by force alone, for it is precisely force itself which is wanting to those amongst us who are threatened by this eventuality. If it were not so, the production in which others are now engaged would not present us with any problem at all.

Does this mean then that all we can do is to bow before the inevitable march of events over which we have no control, and to accept perhaps as a just retribution the reduction at some time in the future of this ancient continent of Europe to the status which her own enterprises have too often forced upon other nations ? Such a possibility is far from desirable not only for Europe itself but for the whole human race. Moreover, however grave a threat it may be, it seems possible to avoid it, at least under certain conditions. To bring these conditions into being is indeed one of the major tasks of our civilization.

The ruthless expansion of vigorous civilizations among peoples less advanced and less powerful has brought spiritual ruin in its train. Even to-day, a mind with any penetration can scarcely fail to feel profoundly saddened as it contemplates values uprooted and suppressed when they might have been preserved and developed in the cycle of growth of a happier civilization. But it is no exaggeration to say that it would be a disaster if the values represented by the peoples of our ancient European civilization were to be repudiated and virtually suppressed by the incoming tide of human groups who are technically more advanced and who might prove as heedless in their conquests as all the great conquerors of the past. For numerous as its defects and faults undoubtedly have been, this ancient European civilization possesses and continues still to possess a mind attuned to the realities of the human situation and also, it must be said, a fermentation of the leaven of the Gospel in the mass of earthly existence hitherto unparalleled in any other civilization. Moreover, this fact provides one of our valid reasons for facing the future with hope.

But the European community of peoples cannot henceforth put its trust in passive hopes and wishful thinking. There is nothing inevitable in the historical process if human consciousness and the resources of the human heart exert themselves in an endeavour to stave off the threat. But they must exert themselves to the full. The nations who are linked together because they have a common source of spiritual energy, have new duties towards one another. It is of the utmost importance that we should be able to appreciate what these duties are and that we should all resolve wholeheartedly to fulfil them.

It is unlikely that the solution of our problems and the preservation of our common civilization can be secured merely by an effort to assure material equality among the nations, each receiving a kind of potential of progress in science, technics and industry, proportioned to its importance in the whole community. This is not the way to act in the sphere of human affairs. It is essential to leave each nation free, as far as is possible, to make its own efforts in accordance with the resources of its own genius, and to a greater or lesser extent according as it is more or less attracted to achievements in this order. A common and rationally co-ordinated plan of work would certainly be a better solution. Even if all the nations cannot organize an original and creative effort in all the fields of modern research and technical progress, it is quite certain that each can do some useful work in one active sector and bring its own authentic contribution by means of its own creative powers. It would doubtless be fanciful to imagine a perfect organization ready for action emerging from the deliberations of a congress. Yet little by little, civilized man seems to be groping towards something of the kind. God grant that partisan prejudices may not prove too great a drag on the progress of all towards this common goal!

But perhaps this is not the main essential. In spite of any organization, however excellent, the differences in their respective situations cannot fail to re-emerge among the nations who thus attempt to strengthen their mutual ties. If we confine ourselves to the plane of material resources, these differences will always be found to have a potentially decisive effect. Much may certainly be done to avoid these inequalities in the distribution of power. Nevertheless it will still remain a fact that the sources of power will be more easily available to some than to others. It is in this connection probably that something quite new in the field of human relations needs to be devised, a kind of politics of generosity in fact. We know already that in certain spheres, the economic for instance, such a policy has become a practical necessity. To-day nothing will function correctly in a worldwide economic system if the latter is left to develop on the basis of the purely mechanical principles of the past. This economic system must be prevented from becoming entangled in its own too rigid mechanisms, by an increasing provision of goods and services without payment. The United States have understood this and so have taken various measures to inaugurate a " gift economy". The philosophical meaning and the spiritual significance of this fact are of greater importance than may appear at first sight. The need for, and the existence of, these methods of giving, of generosity will doubtless soon become an almost universal condition in the world of the future, not only in the economic sphere but in far wider fields of human relationships. It may even be that eventually it will imprint new characteristics upon the spiritual relations of mankind. We must hope that this will indeed be the case.

We must not think of course that we can be content with a one way traffic in generosity, the initiators of this policy on one side and the beneficiaries on the other. This would very soon lead to a form of parasitism as destructive in its effects as suppression by force. But it is possible to discover among nations as among individuals, examples of reciprocal generosity exercised in various spheres and ensuring that all will profit by being called upon to make that effort without which there cannot be any genuine human community.

Ideas such as these are perhaps very Utopian in a hard world where problems of material power still confront us in so brutal a fashion, in a world too where the spirit of war continues to smoulder like a fire that may break into flames at any moment. Yet these are the very ideas which harmonize most closely with our Catholic Faith. These are the ideas which demand to be seriously considered as soon as it is clearly seen that there is probably no other way open to us if we wish to preserve our common civilization.

Such then is our task. It will perhaps be said to our credit that we gave the world a new form of human unity, more deeply marked by the liberty of the spirit than could ever be the case if our fate were left to the blind process of historical destiny or to decisions based upon force.

CHAPTER 4

The Universe of Science and Philosophy

SCIENCE attempts to give us a vision of the universe worthy of intellect, which began to appear upon our planet with the advent of man. We know enough history to appreciate the importance of what it has revealed to us. A little more than two thousand years ago, the Greeks undertook the construction of an already partly rational synthesis of the world as perceived by the senses. We shall begin by recalling the main outlines of that first system of thought, if only to help us to see more clearly where we stand to-day.

The ancient cosmologies occasionally spoke of the boundless universe. But in actual fact, thought limited itself almost entirely to the space occupied by the solar system. The universe had an absolute centre, our planet. Around the latter, celestial orbs, made of a substance having nothing in common with the matter of our earth, carried the stars and ordered their circular, uniform movements. They were thought to be set in motion by mysterious and inexhaustible motor forces, derived from cosmic spirits infinitely superior to human beings. Beyond Saturn, the last of the planets, the last of the orbs bore the fixed stars. Outside of the crystal vault there was nothing and the word 'space' ceased to have any meaning.

The terrestrial world was composed of four elements : earth, water, air and fire were thought to be the basis of the whole structure. Together with the influences emanating from the stars, beginning with that of the radiation of light, these primary entities were considered to be the cause of all earthly phenomena.

A peculiar meteorology attempted to explain a body of more or less heterogeneous data. Once this was done, the formation of observable metals and minerals and then that of living organisms, was related to the qualitative grouping of the elements. Living organisms themselves were dealt with by a still very summary biology, which saw in each living species a permanent structure in act, controlling in a uniform and invariable manner, the constant coming into being of new individuals in their successive generations and their cycle of life and death. Mankind itself, as Aristotle thought, was bound by this condition. In mankind a permanent essence fulfils itself, it is stable and always identical, and the destinies of individuals, generations and nations are nothing more than mere fluctuations with no genuine significance of their own. In the Greek cosmos as it was seen by this early science and summarized by philosophy, everything is resolved in the perception of a harmony, beautiful no doubt, but completely static.

In this harmony, man has his place at the summit of all earthly existence. Nevertheless his is a subordinate and inferior rank in the cosmic hierarchy of that universe of heavenly bodies and spirits which haunted the philosophy of the Greeks. Ideas such as these were for long the staples of the Western mind. They still survived almost in their entirety at the beginning of the sixteenth century. The new advances in scientific thought in the past few centuries have radically altered all this. The skies of the ancient world have opened to reveal spaces involving time factors reckoned in hundreds of millions of light-years. The wonder of the teeming spiral nebulae presents us with the problem of the expanding universe. The " Copernican revolution " has made us recognize that the earth is a planet moving round the sun, and, by the same token, the universe has been revealed to us as boundless with its centre nowhere. The substance of which the stars are made is no different from that of which we are made. The whole world of sensible reality rests on identical foundations: molecules, atoms and lower still, those primary particles of which we still know so little. The configuration of heavenly bodies —single stars, the solar system, stellar groups, nebulae, the whole cosmos—is organized by laws governing the distribution of matter. These laws are essentially at one with those which determine the behaviour of material systems on this planet.

Further, the sciences of matter have revealed to us the continuous series of increasingly complex structures, which includes the primary particles at one end of the scale and the large molecules of organic chemistry at the other. We are beginning to be fairly familiar with the range of inanimate species and we realize that we are now groping our way across the threshold which leads to a sure knowledge of the structures responsible for the primary processes of life itself. We have not yet grasped the truth of the matter, but the human mind is drawing its net ever closer and there is no reason to suppose that we shall not succeed in discovering this mysterious secret at the heart of things.

We now have a clear picture of the evolution of the manifold forms in which life unfolds itself, even in the case of species which to the outward eye appear static and which the Greek view of the cosmos held to be fixed in an everlasting harmonious system. We have, broadly speaking, unravelled the history of the earth and our thought is dominated by the concepts of biological evolution. That the latter is a fact we have no doubt and our analyses are already probing the depths of its mechanisms, whilst our syntheses attempt to tell the full story of this emergent evolution and to retrace in greater detail the history of the vertebrates whose achievements we can now follow step by step. We perhaps see in these triumphs a harmonious progression, although so many riddles still haunt the minds of those who study biological phenomena in any detail. But that evolution is a successful undertaking there can be no question. Its triumphs are glorious but never complete. Biology shows us a world of reality struggling both to endure and to be transformed, a world of being destined to a far nobler fate than that of meaningless fluctuations about an eternal archetype. Effort and chance add their quota to what has already been gained and to such good effect that man himself is the ultimate outcome.

All this implies a new view of the human situation. Man is, in a certain sense, a mere episode if we consider the vast sidereal expanses which envelop the tiny space in which we have our earthly abode, or if we think of those immense aeons of time of which our historic millennia are a mere minute fraction, yet he possesses the privilege of a unique activity. Man is no longer what the ancient world conceived him to be—the highest of earthly creatures yet far inferior to the stars in their glory and divinity. Now man knows that nothing of which he has experience is equal to himself. The astral hierarchies of the past have vanished and their chimerical power has ceased to dominate mankind. Creation in travail, nature giving birth to living things have revealed themselves as placing in the hands of the man whom they have brought into being, the resources of a historical process through which he himself evolves, the resources of civilization, culture, consciousness, and perhaps too of violence and doubt.

Man then must realize that he is free and alone in the possession of this conscious power which moves ever forward as the centuries roll by. There is nothing between him and the absolute problem of this ocean of reality which we now know our universe to be, and man must confront it face to face. We are now convinced that in the universe there is nothing outside ourselves whose task it is to define the elements of a solution to the human problem. True, we are conditioned and in a great number of ways, by all the necessities of our evolution, yet we are not slaves. Scientific inquiry has given us a clearer realization of this truth and presents us with the great and glorious responsibility of bringing into existence realities which the universe itself has not yet produced.

Science and the Education of the human Mind

This picture of things as they are is sufficient to arouse these thoughts in us. Yet science does not confine itself to enlightening man concerning the kind of cosmic structure which he himself is. It is also a type of education and inner transformation of this structure. It has exercised its educative power energetically for the past few centuries, and although it is possible to say hard things about this type of education, it exists and has had a profound effect on a large number of people and, through those whom it has trained to accept its ideals in all their fullness, its influence has been extended indirectly to the whole of modern society. It is especially important therefore to look squarely at what has taken place and to consider what new developments science has introduced into our way of life.

Science insists on intellectual integrity

The rise of the scientific spirit among the Greeks—and how admirable it was, in spite of its postulates as our present state of knowledge reveals them to us—seems to have been due to an amazingly lively curiosity and a virile, noble and distinguished lucidity of mind. Some of its memorials still endure in all their wonder and agelessness. Other passions and other virtues seem to have presided at the birth of the scientific spirit of which we are the direct heirs. All things considered, it appears necessary to give pride of place to a great and almost painful insistence on the integrity of thought when face to face with things. This basic characteristic does not explain all, but it dominates the whole picture.

We may find it somewhat difficult nowadays to recapture the

spirit of those who were the fathers of modern science, and to understand the kind of spiritual drama of which their brilliant ventures were the outcome. In the first place we must realize that they had not only to continue what the Greeks had begun, but also to break new ground. The scientific mind had to set out on a new journey and this in a world where there were intellectual difficulties to be faced, precisely because it was a world in which the life of the intellect had many successes to its credit but of quite a different order from that of science. The thinkers of those great centuries of thought—our European Middle Ages —were the heirs of the Greek concept of the cosmos and they were content with it. Apart from a few individuals in excessive isolation—such as Roger Bacon and perhaps still more Albert the Great who had what, for his time, was an admirable sense of the implications of positive knowledge—the medieval mind developed in the sphere of speculation and left in the background all thought of any careful study of the obscure details of the sensible universe. But gradually a feeling of uneasiness began to arise in the depths of the European mind and—be it noted—long before the great ventures of Galileo or Descartes. It was realized that man's knowledge of what lay before his very eyes was still restricted and that his understanding of such things was defective. Men became convinced that mere discussion at the conceptual level was no remedy for the lack of communication with nature herself. It was essential to plunge once again into the heart of phenomena in the raw, to puzzle out the confused babbling of a reality which the concepts already in use were powerless to grasp or to interpret. Thought groped its way forward slowly and painfully and sometimes dramatically. The remarkable thing about these early efforts is the almost passionate way in which they were pursued. The men who, from the fourteenth to the sixteenth century, were the first to go into action—Roger Bacon, Jean Buridan, Nicole Oresme, Leonardo da Vinci—made almost no discoveries at all. Yet on the plane of thought, seeking to renew contact between the all-conquering intellect and physical reality, they had to break with all the habits of mind which were sanctioned by a routine and convenient cosmology. In doing this, they were not only not understood by others, but sometimes failed to understand themselves completely. But they did discern in reality something which the human intellect still failed to recognize, and they were fully conscious of the fact that the mind could *no longer* remain satisfied with this state of affairs. If truth defaulted here, and the intellect refused to be concerned about it in spite of due warning, then the cause of truth was lost everywhere, for the lack of intellectual integrity would gradually corrupt everything.

Those who first lived through all this certainly did not argue in this way. They did not necessarily make explicit judgments in these terms. But they lived out these convictions in their lives, and by so doing rooted them deeply in our own scientific mind. Once and for all they trained the mind, when in the presence of physical experience, to accept a degree of responsibility greater than man had ever before known. The acquisition of truth, already so widespread in the spheres of philosophical wisdom and theological meditation upon the teachings of faith, had never demanded so detailed and sustained an effort, at least in regard to the humblest objects on our mental horizon. To learn to see, to learn to respect (whatever the cost) the things of which we have only caught a glimpse, to give accurate descriptions, to check every detail, to verify all mental conceptions by the test of facts, to keep clear of all premature speculations and to turn back to concrete reality so solid and unyielding, this is the discipline man patiently learned even before he possessed the means for achieving the great triumphs which only came at a later date. Let us be frank, integrity such as this, research and talk of further research, cost men dearly. Yet so irresistible is the call to knowledge that men were found willing to pay the price. Sometimes the price they paid was the disruption and breakdown of systems of thought that had become too facile. They paid with the heavy tribute of violence, the violence which held them in its grip and the violence they suffered at the hands of others. Too often the price they paid was their own failure to recognize the wealth of divine and human truths which should have been preserved and might well have harmonized superbly with the new intellectual movements these men were inaugurating. Unfortunately, the chief custodians of this wealth all but failed to understand them. To-day, the historian will doubtless regret that so many cleavages were found necessary, so many struggles too, before this fact could be clearly seen. However profound our regret may be, it must not abolish our admiration for those who left us such an example in this great spiritual crisis.

Scientific thought therefore succeeded in making this difficult ideal of the will to intellectual integrity the foundation of its existence in our times. The integrity of positive knowledge has been its cherished ideal. On the primary level of inanimate nature, it has succeeded in establishing systematic and all-embracing techniques to ensure this integrity. The disciplines of the mathematization of phenomena and of methodical experiment which have come down to us enriched and perfected during the course of the centuries are the first-fruits of these techniques. The establishment of free research and the free communication of results, and of the disinterested checking of truth by truth itself—alas, these established customs are to-day threatened with profound modifications—were the second and no less essential achievement. So modern science in its growth has taught something genuinely new to man—a sense of and a new respect for himself and for the universe, based on the love of truth; it is certainly a fact that of this truth he always remains profoundly ignorant, yet he seeks it with increasing zeal, for its own sake and wherever it may be found. Those who, when speaking of these lessons which science has taught us, content themselves with pointing out the many and inevitable lapses which have followed in the train of this great forward movement, fail to maintain a just proportion in their judgments. Seen as a whole and over the centuries, science has done magnificent work towards educating man to be truly himself.

Technical enterprise—its success and significance

As we have already said, this fundamental characteristic is not the whole story. Science is and has always desired to be a discipline in the field of knowledge. This fact is certainly primary and the quest of truth has remained the first law of science. We cannot fail to recognize that this is an essential feature which Greek science did not possess in anything like the same degree. Sometimes, in an effort to facilitate thought, a distinction is made between science, having as its sole object the disinterested knowledge of things, and technics, understood as the mere utilitarian application of knowledge pure and simple, and by the same token as foreign to science as such. It is obvious that gross misunderstandings, which it is not our intention to revive, are thus eliminated. Research is not the industrial or military application of scientific investigation. But this argument does not seem to give an adequate view of the truth concerning modern science.

For our condition in relation to reality is such that we must take practical measures if we are to acquire knowledge, we must introduce some modification into reality even while we are probing its own characteristic structures. The experimental method which we use as the basis of our knowledge always acts in this kind of way, and what takes place in the case of each particle of knowledge which we acquire, is also found in the overall conditions of science. Further progress requires the technical application of science. The laboratory itself needs industrial production and the effective interaction of these two realities cannot be expressed in the terms of any over-simplified explanation. Hence in the field of science as such, to act and to perceive are moments which are not only coordinate and complementary but also indefinably and mutually effective. We never observe nature so well as when we observe the practical uses to which we put it.

This, too, was realized by the men to whom we owe the rise of modern science. They foresaw that science would be both a journey into the truth concerning the things of which we have experience, a victory over nature, and also ultimately a means of transforming the world, beginning with the world of man's own self. I shall give only one quotation, but it sums up all that was said and foreseen at the period when the present scientific era was coming into being. It is from the sixth section of Descartes' *Discours de la Methode*.

As soon as I had acquired a few general notions concerning physics and, beginning to test them in divers particular difficulties, had noticed whither they might lead and how much they differed from the principles hitherto in use, I considered that I could not keep them hidden without sinning gravely against the law which obliges us to procure as far as in us lies the general good of all men. For they made me see that it is possible to acquire knowledge which may be very useful in daily life, and that, in the place of the speculative philosophy which is taught in the schools, a practical one may be found, by means of which, knowing the power and the action of fire, water, air, the stars, the heavens and all the other bodies which surround us, as clearly as we know the divers trades of our artisans, we might employ them in like fashion in all the uses proper to them and thus make ourselves as it were the masters and the possessors of nature, the which is not only to be desired for the invention of a great number of contrivances which would bring it about that we should enjoy without going to any pains the fruits of the earth and all the conveniences that are found therein, but also and principally for the preservation of health, which, it cannot be doubted, is the greatest of all benefits and the foundation of all others in this life . . . : mankind might be delivered from a host of disorders both of body and mind and even maybe of the weakness of old age, if we possessed sufficient knowledge of their causes and of all the remedies with which nature has provided us.

Thus, the man who most passionately desired the highest degree of integrity in the field of natural knowledge at the service of truth, equally desired, by the same indivisible act of his will, a system of practical applications, once knowledge had finally become genuine and certain. Science proclaims its ability to transform reality, and modern man, ever since he first came into contact with science has been attracted by its demiurgic power and desired to make use of it. It is therefore part of man's whole vocation to advance strenuously towards the fulfilment of all his potentialities and to progress both in knowledge and in practical achievement. In fact, a remarkable material revolution has taken place in the world as a result of man's scientific adventure. The scientific mind foresaw this revolution from the beginning. It waited and hoped for it. In willing its own existence it chose to accept the revolution on behalf of mankind. In a certain sense, it has claimed for itself all the achievements of this forward movement. It may be all to the good that one day the scientific mind should more fully acknowledge as its own the difficulties and problems which the passage of time has shown are bound up with it. But more of this later.

In any case, science contributes to man's education in this field also. It makes him aware of creative powers which were never so clearly revealed by previous intellectual movements. When man faces the world of infinite possibilities opened to him by the range and the thought of new fields of knowledge, he is given not only the task of contemplating and accepting what we may call a ready-made body of truth concerning the nature of things, but also the duty of contributing something of himself so that these new fields of knowledge may exist in fact. He only receives if he for his part gives something of what he possesses. The world must be *made* intelligible. All the resources of truth it offers us will be as nothing at the human level so long as the methodic activities of the mind do not turn them to account by revealing truth in the production of new lines of thought. We must also make the world by the use of our reason a better and more beautiful place than it already is. We may even say that if the human mind were to measure fully up to nature as it offers itself to us, then the movement of scientific progress should aim at the transformation of the whole of existence as we now know it into a fabric as vast as the universe itself. The most wonderful of our modern machines are only a very incomplete and remote approximation to this renewal of reality through thought and the exercise of reason. Yet it is enough that we are able to see approximations like these for us to perceive, at least in germ, the undeniable power of man. Once this power has been recognized, what is surprising is not that it should exist but that it should do so in so restricted a fashion, when all is said and done, by comparison with the enormous dead weight of the material world it has to confront. One might almost think that there is an unfair disproportion between the universe as it already is with the tremendous mission it seems to be entrusting to us, and the poverty of the means with which it provides us in making us the beings we in fact are.

These educational factors so deeply embedded in the scientific consciousness are far from being its exclusive possession. Not only the men of science and the research workers but also the communities of mankind have their share in the new knowledge. There is no point in drawing attention to the aspects of these facts which have become common property. The austere disciplines of truth have hardly spread at all, whilst the sense of adventure and of progress is more general. On the other hand, we must emphasize the fact that the forward movement of the scientific mind has had a kind of harmonic relation to all the deliverances of the life of the mind during the period when science was seeking and finding itself. It is only natural that this should be so and that scientific enterprise should correspond to a certain extent with man's researches on all planes, civil life, religion, art, philosophical thought. We must look upon science as a contribution, in some respects a major and predominant contribution, to the creation of a new style of thought which, since the end of the Middle Ages, Western man has felt an irresistible urge to inaugurate. At this level, all the great human phenomena have common roots, and the scientific mind itself is the bearer of a whole implicit doctrine concerning the conditions under which the historical process has now placed the life of the intellect.

Science and Philosophy

Once this has been said, we must underline the fact that the development of science in its modern form has brought about for the mind in its philosophical approach to science, a profound transformation of the philosophical situation itself. Before this development, the world of thought associated, or at least claimed to associate in the concrete unity of knowledge, both what we to-day call positive science and what we call philosophy. The term " philosophy " had long existed, but it meant at one and the same time the methodical survey of the data of experience, and reflexion which, by dealing with the primary problems of understanding, attempts a synthesis of this understanding. For the Greeks and for the men of the Middle Ages, true philosophy is knowledge and an all-embracing knowledge. In spite of certain warnings already present in Plato's teaching and in spite of the irrelevancy of mathematics in the Aristotelian tradition, it was agreed in the past that scientific knowledge was one with the work of philosophy, for the latter was nothing but the growth of reasoning and of all reasoning. The philosopher considered himself at home in every order of knowledge, in every field where a methodical system of thought was employed. The development of modern science obliges us to revise this estimate of the status of mind.

A necessary Distinction

Scientific endeavour is one thing, the traditional philosophical attitude of reason is another. The ancient synthesis contains an ambiguity. Positive evidence is only represented in it at the level of sense knowledge coordinating the daily experiences of things and of the world. Reason is all but limited to reflexive (and at times very profound) meditation on this primary food of the mind in quest of knowledge. Modern science was only able to organize itself by unravelling this complex which, under the species of the old peripatetic physics laid claim to nothing less than permanent status. For the relatively static and largely confused deliverances of ordinary experience common to all of us, science proposed to substitute a knowledge derived from accurate, critical, elaborate and subtle observation, and a progression towards ever wider fields of perception, a movement drawing us ever deeper into the heart of things. For the rational processes of constructive speculation and the exclusively reflexive development of concepts, science substituted mathematical rationalization and the whole apparatus of a strictly deductive investigation. All these things forced scientific practice to differ from the customary methods of philosophical thought.

The division between these two rational functions begins to appear in the seventeenth century. Certain great protagonists of modern science at that time were still great philosophers, Descartes and Leibniz for instance. Since them the number of philosophers engaged in scientific study has become increasingly smaller. Conversely, serious and genuinely philosophical reflexion has been increasingly uncommon among scientists. It is impossible to do everything at once. Genius itself is obliged to take into account the constitution of the human reason which insists upon the distinction between our modern scientific discipline and the purposes of philosophical endeavour. To use a metaphor, the stock upon which the intellect grows is common to both but different branches of rational thought have inevitably developed from it.

This dualism now clearly marked in the realm of the mind, is therefore both a natural fact and a historical achievement which cannot be discarded. Science may originate to a certain extent from a philosophy, whilst the scientist's method of procedure may contain a kind of implicit philosophy. Or again, science may give rise to a philosophy and provide it with materials. Doubtless it is destined in part to do this. But science is something other than a distinct and explicit philosophical act. For its part, philosophy is well aware that it is wasting its time if it mimics science and builds up its own structure as though its proper task were to go through the motions of science in an effort to explore some universe or other unknown to science. In this connection it might even be said that the existence of science teaches philosophy to elect to be something quite different from the scientific knowledge of a thing. If we face the facts squarely, philosophy can only be the scientific knowledge of a thing in a metaphorical sense, given the present situation in the life of the mind. Such knowledge is the prerogative of science and must be left in its possession. Philosophy is intrinsically of another order.

Philosophy considered from the point of view of the scientific Consciousness

It remains then to say what philosophy really is. We may state

—and nowadays with greater assurance—that at the lowest estimate it is the act of free reflexion. But the simplicity of this definition must not be allowed to mislead us. Doubtless we all very frequently find ourselves reflecting in a rough and ready sort of way. Daily life as well as science cannot do without such careful looking back over the ground that we have covered in our activities, nor without thoughtful meditation on the problems that arise. Scientific thought instinctively attempts to integrate its findings and to group its results so that they may be aids to the mind in search of understanding. This is already to enter in some sort the universe of the philosopher. Thus, in this respect, like Monsieur Jourdain, we often find that we are already philosophers without knowing it or bothering our heads about it. This is no doubt because the background of the intellect is in a sense necessarily philosophical. But philosophy in the full meaning of the term is not content with these immediate and episodic reflective activities.

For philosophy, reflexion must be coterminous with life itself, grasped in all its rich and complex profusion of experiences. We must not even restrict philosophy to life alone, for it must attempt to make contact with the vast community of mankind in the long process of its history, the diversity of its cultures, the multitude of its societies and institutions. Even this is not enough. Philosophy must confront the indeterminate in our experience, even although we already know that it is beyond the range of all perception and never ceases to thwart our efforts to reach conclusions concerning any aspect whatsoever of its being. Philosophy is reflexion in search of itself and having a total view as its constant aim in spite of the fact that we cannot say that such a view is absolutely certain to be reached by a mind which, in actual fact, discovers in its efforts to attain to it, that it has no complete knowledge of anything.

Further, philosophy is the act of free reflexion. Any man

who is truly a man knows that this liberty is always hard to come by, and alas ! always uncertain and threatened. We have to be free not only in order to think, but also in the act of thinking. When the mind allows itself to be absorbed in the knowledge and doctrines which nourish it, philosophy ceases to exist. The difficulty is to maintain our mastery over all that has to be accepted and welcomed. Everything in life must be accepted and cherished, not in order to abandon ourselves to it, but so that we may rise above it and so grasp its substance. Wisdom does not disdain the passive sides of man's nature. For all we know, she is not absent even in those moods of violence which convulse our being. But in their presence she strives to be independent of them and to see them clearly as they are, so far as this is possible.

Philosophy is a hard school. It is understandable that time and continual effort are needed, not indeed in the beginning, for we all possess in ourselves all that is needed to make a start, but rather to reach the deep levels of those possibilities which lie open to us. The task which the philosophers have always set themselves is to pursue reflexion to the very end. Such is their vocation and, once the human mind is sufficiently mature, it obliges them to allow scientific inquiry to go forward on its own account, whilst the philosopher disclaims any intention of directly doing its work. If philosophy in the past has been the matrix of the sciences, it is essential that the organism to which it has given birth should one day fulfil its own destiny independently and so, in return, liberate and purify a function to which it itself is in debt. . . .

Philosophy is always indispensable to those who have received a scientific Culture

It is true that there are risks attached to this liberation of philosophical energy. Scientific thought has often acted as though the world of scientific knowledge in achieving a status of its own, has thereby rendered meaningless the processes of pure reflexion. Science has sometimes wondered why it should not finally undertake the responsibility of integrating itself and of integrating everything into itself, without further reference to a philosophy which intends to continue its work by methods quite other than those of science. Sometimes even, philosophical reflexion itself has been content to exist merely in order to reach this same conclusion. So great is the difficulty human thought experiences in recognizing the value of anything that transcends its customary certainties! To-day, however, all of us have within ourselves the wherewithal to rebut the arguments which claim that the attitude of philosophy should be eliminated once and for all and its place taken by the scientific method.

It is true that, especially during the last century, scientific thought enjoyed a happy and, as far as philosophy was concerned, an easy period. This good fortune, this smooth passage now seem to have been partly the result of a certain lack of awareness. But they were also the natural concomitant of the early youth of science at the beginning of its movement of expansion and without any major problems. The philosophical implications of science's farewell to philosophy merely bore witness to a movement full of self-confidence, persuaded by its first results that it would continue to be successful, and asking for nothing more than to go its own way in complete freedom. Everything now points to the fact that this first period is nearing its close.

The human Elements and their effect on scientific Expansion
The difficulties they cause

We will start with the most obvious facts. So long as the results of scientific enterprise could be considered as still insignificant in comparison with the sum total of human existence, the scientific consciousness was spared certain problems. The most considerable difficulty in the past was the human problem raised by that industrial expansion for which the way was opened by the techniques made possible by scientific progress. At first at least, it seemed theoretically a simple problem, and the scientific conscience by and large was satisfied with what it considered to be adequate solutions, somewhat summary though they were. On the one hand, scientific progress declared that it was not technics still less industrial enterprise. On the other hand, a spirit of vigorous optimism—largely justifiable at first sight—gave rise to the view that progress would bring almost nothing but good in its train. The production of wealth would increase and all classes of society would soon be in comfortable circumstances. The end of the eighteenth century which saw the invention of the steam engine, was also the period of those economic doctrines according to which the successful combination of technical possibilities, the freedom of enterprise and of trade, and finally the unwritten laws which nature automatically imposes upon the interplay of human activities, would of itself bring into being a type of society far superior to any that had gone before. These hopes have not been proved entirely false by the event. But in actual fact, the beginning of the nineteenth century saw also the inevitable formation of the modern proletariat. This was enough to introduce profound modifications of thought in the field of political economy. Yet the scientific conscience seems hardly to have been affected at the time by the data of this unexpected sequel. Since that time, human problems have increased in magnitude, and now the implications of science are seen to concern them so immediately that the scientific conscience must take them into consideration. Let it be said to his credit, that the scientist has not shirked this duty.

Broadly speaking, we may say that two orders of facts now claim the attention of the scientific consciousness. One is that of the utilization of science for destructive ends, the other is the threat of the restraints imposed upon scientific integrity itself by influences—or if we prefer, by necessities—external to science itself, and especially those of a political nature, using this word in a fairly wide sense. Between these two orders, there are close connexions. In short, they are but two aspects of the challenge presented to science by its human context.

Science and the Threat of Destruction through human Agency

There is no point in emphasizing the problems raised by the use of science for destructive ends. The fact that a considerable proportion of scientific research is now directed by military aims is sufficiently well known to us all, underlined as it is by the atomic bombardments which destroyed Hiroshima and Nagasaki in August, 1945. A decade has passed since then and we know that there has been no general improvement in the situation. While we scarcely give the matter a thought or, if we do, only in a half-hearted way, fate marches on. To-day we cannot say whether mankind will have wisdom enough to ward off its threats or whether it may not be necessary for the same question to be put to us in a still more terrifying manner. We can only say that if it is put to us again, it will probably be in terms of the powers man has at his disposal at both ends of the scale of inanimate substances— matter as convertible into energy and as a substratum for the most elementary forms of life (see p. 92). It may well be that in these we possess two ways of bringing about mass slaughter without yet knowing whether there may not be a crucial moment when the magnitude of the destructive forces threatens to escape completely from our control and predictions. It would seem that this is a point worthy of a little reflexion.

The Integrity of Science threatened by political Events

Once we have stated that this is the case, we must give a clearer account of this set of problems than is commonly done, for it has a direct bearing on the integrity of science. Two facts stand out. In the first place, an increasing amount of scientific research is now affected by a " discipline of the secret " imposed by administrative authorities whose sphere of competence is ultimately political and not scientific. This policy is adopted because of the political and not the intrinsically scientific repercussions of these branches of research. It is true that the origins of this practice are by no means modern, but at present, what used to be a passing phase tends to become a permanent institution. It is no longer simply a question of a few relatively unimportant sectors concerned with incidental practical applications rather than essential facts and principles. The sectors affected by these measures are the most fundamental ones— physics, biology, and on occasion even mathematics. How could it be otherwise at the very time when it is essential to know the behaviour of the nuclear sources of energy and the immediate substructures of life itself, at a time when the theorems of the Theory of Games are applied to the organization of the Berlin air-lift ? Free communication of results and freedom of action in research are both therefore things of the past. Contrary to what is sometimes thought, the immediate consequences of this policy are quite far-reaching. Every single administrative decision involves the machinery of a police force and the latter is all the more strict in that the activity to be placed under control is of itself the freest of all. I am not maintaining that in a world like ours the traditional freedom to do what we like just as we like can still be called wise. Nor have I any ready made solution to the problem. I have no competence in this sphere. But neither do I think that it is good for the scientific community to write off its own liberty in order to allow only those communities whose business is warfare the freedom to assert their own will and to bend to their own purposes minds set apart for the discovery of truth.

Nor is this all. It is also a fact that the period in which we live finds it increasingly difficult to do without collective ideologies aiming to control the individual's way of life as well as the general cultural patterns, and ultimately tending to be the inner soul of political structures. At a certain level it would even be less than true to say that ideology is merely an instrument of power. In a sense, ideology is power itself. This power-ideology aims to integrate scientific thought in its own way by imposing once and for all upon the scientific consciousness doctrines which would be unlikely greatly to interest science if left to itself. We all of us are aware of facts which are symptomatic for us of such a questionable linking of science and politics. But I should be very surprised if at this moment we are all thinking of the same facts. As far as politics are concerned, we are all sadly inadequate and too inclined to consider only the defects of our adversaries without apparently being affected by or even guessing at those of our own side. Here again I do not pretend to judge but to begin by stating the facts. It may even perhaps be in a sense legitimate to associate to some extent in our minds scientific thought and political doctrines. The world of thought is not divided into separate and radically alien provinces. Why should there not be valid relationships between them not only in regard to the truths which are asserted but also in regard to the style of thought which the intellect adopts? Yet neither do I think that the abandonment of scientific freedom in exchange for a brutal or insidious control of science by politics can have any desirable results for mankind in the future.

In circumstances where it is faced by unforeseen developments and an actual evolution in the concrete situation, which threatens to enslave it to the purposes of death or else to disintegrate the fundamental principles of its spiritual vitality, the scientific consciousness is called upon to regain possession of itself and to address itself to the task of preserving its own inheritance. This is tantamount to saying that it must once again seek a philosophy, for only a philosophical attitude can unravel these problems. The specifics of the past are no longer sufficient now that the mere impulses to which we have been accustomed run the risk of producing nothing but chaos, now that, in a word, it is not only essential to acquire or develop knowledge by the customary methods, but above all to realize where we stand and to understand what is at stake.

The undermining of the classical Certitudes of Science from within

To this complex of human implications so well calculated to give rise again to philosophical reflexion, there now corresponds another philosophical requirement. It is less obvious but more imperative, and it comes from within scientific thought itself in the full tide of its development. For, in the light of this development, the scientific mind is now discovering a whole new and unexpected order of problems, problems to which the present advances of science can indeed lead the mind, but which, once they have arisen, seem impossible to master without efforts of thought made possible only by philosophical energy in the proper sense of the term.

The philosophers seem to have had a presentiment of this. They have doubtless not been the least among those to be impressed by what have been called the "crises" of scientific thought which have arisen since the beginning of the present century; the crisis of the axiomatic in mathematics, the crisis of the revolution in the theoretical concepts of physics. The scientists for their part have been less preoccupied with these crises. They have shown that the disruption of ideas which has taken place is offset by the powerful vitality of science which is responsible for this disruption. In a sense, they say, crises in the conceptual field are of little importance if they are the price to be paid for a renewal of the fertility of science,

But the instinct of the philosophers is sound. At a deeper level, where scientific thought professes to be an educative force, recent developments do demand, whether we like it or not, a revival of philosophical reflexion. The mind in becoming scientific undertakes the obligation not only of integrity in the presence of what is to be known, but also of integrity in respect of the principles which are held to be valid in the pursuit of knowledge. In view of their age-old stability, these principles were willingly accepted as fixed en bloc and as able to establish the human intellect in a perfectly secure mathematical certitude. But the conditions under which science works are now seen to be less simple than this. Even mathematics, whose essence seems to be of such a necessary nature, have not the entirely absolute character which we are automatically led to attribute to them. We know enough physics to be aware that nature does not correspond entirely to our customary conceptions in all their classical rigour. The same is true of time, extension, the interaction of things upon one another, the causal relations of processes. The human mind in observing all this, foresees the possibility of new forms of liberty at its disposal and already sees the rise of new and fascinating ideas. But at the same time, it feels it is approaching a new and unknown realm, of which the intellect as yet knows nothing at all. Even among the men of science, who can boast that here and now he has perfectly understood what the progress of science itself has prompted us to accept as true ?

On the whole, man is discovering more and more clearly that the science whose protagonist and master he is, cannot fix for itself any absolute centre from which thought may range over its whole field, somewhat as ancient astronomy thought it could contemplate the whole extension of the universe from the earth which remained stable in the centre of the whole. The foundations of our science also have their secret workings and gravitational pulls. Its firmest principles are now once again assailed by the indeterminate and the changing. The problem which is raised by this fact is to try to find a way to extract from the indeterminate and the changing, something other than just that uncertainty and disintegration which they run the risk of causing, for so long as the mind is content to remain passive to them. We must stake all upon those truths which are only waiting for new and pure intellectual efforts on our part, in order to come into being. And since the whole of man is here involved, philosophy once again stands upon the horizon. The one great phenomenon of our times is the fact that scientific thought, from within itself and by its own impetus is leading us back to the point where it is essential for the human intellect to wrestle once more naked with the naked truth.

A new spiritual human situation is therefore taking shape in our present circumstances. It is very difficult not to see the increasingly important part scientific thought is destined to play in it. But at the same time, it seems that human consciousness is far from having completed its education. All things to-day, even the most powerful visions of the universe which we are now able to delineate, even the most essential habits of thought which science has succeeded in instilling into the human mind, by the very fact of their increasing growth, finally bring the mind back to the point where the activity of philosophical thought must come to birth, if we wish humanity to continue its existence in this universe.

At such a time as the present, we too often envisage only chaos or even the dark signs of a future ending in ultimate ruin. We must end this chapter by pointing out that in such a human venture as that which confronts us, there is more true order than we suppose. The world of the present in fact offers man—and without there being any question of sacrificing any of the achievements of the past—the opportunity of a new and more mature, more intensive inquiry into his own nature and that of all other things. Let us for the moment think, not of the fruitless discussion of a question to which there is no answer, but of the possibility of a new, lucid and determined thought, opening up the way and giving rise to the new resources of human stability which the future expects of us. To bring this about cannot now be the business of philosophy alone, nor of science alone. It is the business of a coordinated effort on the part of both, or at least of a new dialogue between these two major powers of the human reason. There is no need for me to mention what else it seems to me will be necessary, originating as it does from a higher source. But I can say that there is something supremely noble about these meetings between man and man, when the powers which have grown to adult stature and are masters of their own impulses, learn to converse and to answer one another as equals in the world of the mind in spite of the essential differences which are represented by the values for which each is responsible. We are now dealing with sciences which are well on their way to maturity. We also possess in ourselves the opportunity of inaugurating a philosophical attitude having a clear idea of what its proper functions are. The grave nature of the circumstances which are demanding the maintenance of this science and this philosophical attitude, far from signifying that our enterprise is a total loss, can make us augur that, if we do succeed, our success may indeed be a glorious one. It may well be that we are rediscovering in a new form, in a free and hospitable community of the spirit, that unity which modern man so rightly complains that he has lost.

P. 86. In a letter to the translator, Père Dubarle writes "I mean that matter runs the risk of being dangerous for mankind as a whole both because it can be converted into energy and because of the possibility that it may become living."

CHAPTER 5

THE ATTITUDE OF CHRISTIANITY TO SCIENTIFIC PROGRESS

ONE of the characteristics of our time is the part science is called upon to play. Mankind to-day is not merely anxious to assimilate the increased knowledge made available to us by science, or even to extend research; it is no longer satisfied to exploit in the technical field the practical possibilities to which this knowledge gives access, nor to proceed with a whole programme whose purpose it is to renew the face of the earth and to transform man's condition. To-day mankind promotes science both in its creative and cognitive functions to the dignity of a new philosophical instrument of vital importance for our thought concerning existence. In a sense it is the privilege of modern science to oblige all mankind to ask itself as a body what is its being and destiny. Science no longer limits itself to providing food for individual reflexion. To-day the whole race of men is shaken by its revelations and finds itself faced with a problem which cannot be avoided.

Science is now in possession of everything it needs to inaugurate such a movement of the spirit. In the sphere of knowledge there is a remarkable abundance of research and discovery together with a more far-reaching disclosure of the relative nature of man's idea of the universe. In the sphere of action, the first circuit of world industry with its various human, economic, political and cultural aspects is now closed. This fact, whilst it presents technical problems of a new kind (human endeavour is now seen to be confined within a limited space) is accompanied by the advent of new possibilities which prove that man is far from having plumbed nature to its furthest depths. World organization will have to reckon with nuclear energy and man's remarkable new mastery of biological processes. In every department, enrichment and bewilderment go hand in hand, but they involve the breakdown of human institutions too narrow to contain them. The quantum and relativity theories have forced scientific thought to take on new forms. On the practical plane the situation is less clear, yet the new conditions produced by the evolution of technics are manifestly and increasingly leading mankind towards a new apprenticeship. To-day we need virtues of a new type. The former ones no longer serve as adequate controls for our activity.

Yet science continues to progress with the steady rhythm of a natural phenomenon. This progress itself allows us to anticipate what the future holds in store. We also know, though more or less clearly in different cases, what the knowledge already acquired leads us to expect. To-morrow the atomic nucleus will have no secrets for the human mind, the biological sciences will no longer be shrouded in the obscurity which our present methods are inadequate to dispel. To-morrow mankind will be able to build a new civilization in which an entirely new balance will be struck between man and the machine. The forces of life itself will be mastered to a degree beyond anything now known. Social organisms will thus be transformed. Space travel will probably become possible and may well mark the beginning of a cosmic adventure of which we now have no conception. All this is obviously still in the realm of conjecture. But to-day we know that the passage of time is constantly justifying premonitions based on scientific facts and often with lightning rapidity.

In a word science seems to be implanting in the human mind the germ of a new prophetic power. This prophetic power is asserting itself vigorously to-day and mankind, shaken out of its old habits and impelled forward by the force of its own aspirations, is ceaselessly questioning itself as to its future. It is a well-known, if not remarkable, fact that this spontaneous questioning has its dark side. By and large, science presents itself to modern man as a reality to be admired, as, in a sense, the most manifest of human triumphs, but also as something rather terrifying and full of risks. For the moment, man sees nuclear energy chiefly as a destructive power. The fearful shape of this atomic world so suddenly revealed, stands on the threshold of all our thought concerning mankind in the clutches of rationally organized power. The scientists do not conceal their own fears. At the level of the indiscriminating masses panic needs no encouragement, fostered as it is by a dubious taste for the sensational. Our philosophical awakening, we must admit, is largely based on fear and anxiety. Tragic and optimistic possibilities intermingle in our questioning.

The present situation in Scientific development

Although many people content themselves with an emotional reaction either of uncritical enthusiasm or hopeless anxiety, it seems essential not to allow ourselves to be carried away by the current, but to keep our vision as clear as possible. Our first human task—we shall speak later of the specifically Christian task—is to weigh up the situation. Let us say at once that it seems to us impossible to describe it unless we see the internal development of science in the context of a whole framework of conditions arising from the present state of mankind as it effectively is; and these conditions are what they are, independently for all practical purposes of the actual state of scientific knowledge.

The achievements of science as such. Due allowance having been made for the future development of science, the following are in our view the essential points.

1. *The sciences of matter*. The sciences of matter have almost completed their first cycle. As far as can be judged from certain tendencies in research and from certain affinities in its results, we are not very far, both in the cases of very large and very small bodies, from a complete inventory of their mechanical interactions. The human mind is in the process of grasping the characteristics of the heavens, and of the element, as well as the structure of extension and duration, and this to an extent which it seems will indicate a final stage in research analagous to that which made the ancient cosmologies a final stage in a type of research based on the immediate experience of reality. Mathematics and mechanics are elaborating conclusions drawn from their field of experiment.

At the same time, nuclear energy is putting us in touch, so to speak, with the most powerful sources of the cosmic force which is to be found in inorganic matter. At this initial stage our contact with them is very remote. To the rationalized apparatus of the atomic bomb and the atomic pile correspond, at the other end of the scale of chemical elements, the natural machinery which supplies stellar energy and whose immensity is infinitely beyond our powers. The sun, a relatively small star, is capable of liberating every second and over a period of some ten million years an amount of energy equivalent to that of more than four thousand billions of atomic bombs. There is obviously a considerable margin of possibilities yet to be explored.

Yet in spite of the diminutive character of this triumph, man is disconcerted by the magnitude of the step he has taken: the change in scale is indeed considerable, since from one gramme of suitably chosen matter, some millions of times more can be extracted than from the same weight of the most powerful combustibles known. It seems, fortunately on the whole, that the shock of this transition is attenuated for man in the first place by the magnitude of the technical difficulties involved in the preparation of the necessary apparatus (in particular as regards adequate safety precautions) and then by the comparison under present circumstances of the manufacturing costs of nuclear energy with those of other forms of energy. This monetary arbitrage will presumably not always remain constant. For the time being, it exercises an invaluable moderating influence in respect of the economic and social repercussions of the situation. It is only in the military and political spheres that danger stares us in the face. To this we shall return later. But at this point we can say that the world is still not too bad a place and that it is possible to imagine far more violent ways in which nuclear energy might have burst through the frail crust of the world of mankind. If considered carefully, the chances of assimilating these great possibilities remain very considerable in spite of a certain number of more immediate anxieties.

2. *The sciences of life*. If there are many facts which lead us to think that, as far as the knowledge of matter is concerned, we are nearing the completion of a cycle, everything on the contrary points to the fact that man is only about to inaugurate the true science of life. He has not yet done so, for all the present accumulation of knowledge is in a sense preliminary and may be compared with what was known of the movement of bodies a few centuries ago before Galileo, Descartes and Newton. But knowledge and techniques are obviously approaching maturity. Their results are now at the stage when the parts are all beginning to cohere and to corroborate one another. Enlightened by the converging evidence of biochemical techniques, paleontology and embryology and the empirical findings of genetics and physiology, the human mind will perhaps in the near future be capable of attacking the fundamental problem of the transition from inorganic to organic matter, and also of

discovering a definite solution to it. On that day, a new order of scientific thought will be born.

Yet our biology, empirical though it has been, has acquired certain interesting powers. We are able to exercise considerable influence on the adaptation of a species of livestock to its environment. This in fact means that we have adapted previous methods of domestication and acclimatization, but by beginning to bring our action to bear from within the vital situation. Further, we are able to regulate to a greater or lesser degree according to cases, the phenomena of generation and the mechanisms of heredity. The systematic development of these possibilities, in particular their deliberate exploitation at the human level, has already succeeded in bringing about a number of changes. Medicine, zoology and eugenics are bringing their new practices into force and so oblige us to look at reality in a new light. We need only point out the profound modifications that have occurred in the past few years in current ideas concerning sexual matters. All this doubtless is only a small beginning.

Nevertheless, it is essential here, more than anywhere else to appreciate the precise limits of our achievement, even though the mind experiences the need to prepare for eventualities yet to come. The sciences of life and the techniques derived from them, cannot yet establish beyond question all the certitude and power we too easily think they already possess. Man is not yet master of life itself. He has no clear understanding of it, and his efforts in this sphere show that his powers are of a minor character. Their range increases daily but their repercussions nevertheless remain not too disproportionate to the natural abilities of human consciousness. Much that the ideas of the new biology now enable us to envisage, e.g., the techniques of the deliberate determination of sex, even parthenogenesis, are still beyond human power. We must remember that we anticipate considerably at times in this sphere and are unconsciously tempted to confuse the much humbler realities with our too rosy pictures of the future.

Moreover, there is no need to be frightened by the future or to be impatient with the present. We surmise that biology will one day be a very different science. The time—and it may be short—which has still to elapse before this is the case, seems to be granted to the human mind so that it may grow more mature and prepare itself to welcome a fact of such importance. Here, still more than with atomic energy, we feel the need to reflect and to purify the human soul. Beneath its vague fear of the repercussions of biological knowledge, lies mankind's hope that men will arise capable of reassuring it and of teaching it how to behave in a manner worthy of the power which it is about to possess. This expectation may very possibly be realized, if not to the extent of warding off all harm yet at least sufficiently to preserve mankind from the new evils which it is feared may beset us, and to maintain a general upward movement in human evolution.

3. *Beyond biology.* To speak of a *science* beyond biology is really to speak metaphorically. We do not know, nor are we in a position to guess, the principles of science in the case of a sentient psychical organism, still less in the case of the human psyche. To a greater extent than with biological topics we have to be satisfied with a very external type of empiricism and with the knowledge we derive from the mind's inner consciousness of itself. Even if one day it becomes possible for mankind to acquire in this domain a science in the full sense of the term, this is not likely to happen for a long time to come, and a considerable advance in the field of biological knowledge will be necessary before we are in a position to encompass the mystery of mind.

Yet this external empiricism is in fact developing to a very considerable degree, and obscure though it still is, it does constitute a vast store of knowledge: psycho-somatic conditions of psychical phenomena, behaviour patterns of conscious beings, statistical constants in the collective life of animals and men, spiritual constituents immanent in mental acts, all these already lead our inquiry into a field offering a vast number of opportunities for the more or less systematic development of theory, and a multitude of practical possibilities in consequence. The decisive importance of these researches lies in the fact that they naturally all converge on man himself and make it possible for us to prepare the way for the science of man by investigating whatever subjects his being to laws analogous to those of physics and biology. In respect at least of this material dimension everywhere present in him and conditioning the exercise of his various spiritual activities, man becomes more and more specifically the "local habitation" in which a rationalized form of existence can take shape. Attempts may be made to condition individual evolution and to organize collective life, and perhaps simultaneously. What we now see happening spontaneously and on a small scale, man may attempt to continue deliberately, systematically and on a large scale.

It is a very remarkable contemporary fact that the intellect is actually engaged in acquiring the instruments which will allow a systematic effort to be made in this sphere. The tools for the statistical analysis of human phenomena in particular are now being forged; they are the mechanical devices for the collection and utilization of information, and the great calculating machines. We shall no doubt soon have also apparatus for obtaining predictions in numerical form. The time is not far distant when it will be possible to carry out a systematic programme of inquiries and predictions which will cover the whole of mankind. The machine will do rapidly and accurately what would be beyond the powers of a whole army of calculators using the usual methods of intellectual work. Man's brain is thus being provided with auxiliary mechanisms capable of coping with the material problems of the world. This is but an elementary achievement in face of the difficulties that beset thought when overburdened with material data, but it is an achievement whose consequences for human life may be more numerous than those resulting from the sum total of what has been achieved by the sciences of inorganic matter.

In the last analysis, it is perhaps in this realm of research into a reality superior to that studied by biology that man's gravest risks may prove to lie. To perish suddenly the victim of some stark, physical catastrophe, may not be the worst fate that can befall mankind. To be led by some evil fate hastily to use powers that are only ours in part, in order to shut ourselves up in a kind of universe in which the mind could not live, would be a worse fate than a sudden and violent end. Such is precisely the risk to be run over a period which nothing justifies us in thinking will be short. We shall soon know how to handle the problems of organic matter. The solutions at which we shall arrive will always involve a failure to recognize some aspect of man's nature, the unique character of his psychical organism, or still more, his personal potentialities of intellect and freedom of action. There will then always be a strong temptation to reduce man to the level of these rationally effective solutions rather than to attempt to keep these solutions themselves open to the ultimate dimensions of humanity. A society of men whose problems are solved by an unremitting process of dehumanization, an existence made up of methodically conditioned motions, the powers of criticism and reactivity intentionally inhibited—this is no mere idle fantasy, and we sometimes wonder whether the modern world does not already offer sporadic examples of that degradation of humanity which it would be appalling to see emerge as the final outcome of a science unmindful of realities which still lie partly outside its range.

It is true that here again we should not be too despondent as we look towards the future. The idea of mankind reduced to the conditions of the ant-hill under the heel of some Lord of the World, is a warning rather than an effective possibility. For man has it in him to refuse indefinitely this state of subjugation, and in ways we cannot foresee. If the experiment were tried it would doubtless be seen that the spirit is not so easily quenched. The forces of reflexion and resistance may be quiescent in the individual, they may even stagnate through whole periods of history, but it is very unlikely that man can force them to desert mankind for ever.

But if man is too hasty in his use of the powers he acquires over himself, he risks being forced to assert what is best in his nature under conditions which his own relative stupidity will have made unfavourable, conditions giving birth to conflict and suffering, whereas nothing need prevent him from maintaining these same spiritual values in an infinitely better and happier atmosphere. The dictatorship of a science still only partly developed, an unintelligent determination to organize the world of men along the lines of schemes which, though rational, are still too grossly material, may drive man's spirit either to revolt or to martyrdom, those tragic forms, magnificent and sublime though they are, of man's affirmation of his humanity, but which it would be madness deliberately to provoke.

4. *The New Theoretical approach.* It remains for us to define the present state of science from the theoretical point of view. The situation is complex. It is the result not only of the development of the mathematical sciences but also, on the one hand, of the increasingly obvious influence of a logic which is still in the process of organizing itself as a science, and, on the other hand, of the increasingly firm establishment of a form of mathematical physics, the very idea of which would have seemed singularly daring only a few decades ago. Thus a profound revolution in our understanding of theoretical knowledge is in course of preparation, and to it we must now turn our attention.

Apart from a few specialists, the importance of the rise of symbolical logic and the significance of the relations established between this discipline and mathematics, is usually unrecognized, especially in France. Symbolical logic is quite literally the starting point of a new understanding of the object of theoretical science, of a new organization of the mind's rational capacities. Instead of conceiving of mathematics merely as the science of a datum genuinely encountered in the actuality of an existence independent of the act of thought (quantity, extension, etc.) we are now being led to see it as grasping an object whose existence also requires the fact of the mental process itself. There is no mathematics without the work of thought, beginning with the work of verbal expression whose logic constitutes the specific discipline which must precede all theoretical science. Now at last mathematics enables us to understand, at least in part, the reason for its bewildering fertility, for the manifold forms of spatial or operational models that have evolved within its field in the last fifty years from the elementary bases of Euclidian geometry and ordinary arithmetic. Again—passing beyond a certain number of negative experiences such as the impossibility of constructing a perfect logical system capable of integrating ordinary mathematics—we are beginning to foresee the ultimate possibility of new forms of mathematical intelligibility. The human intellect may still be far from mastering them unmistakably, but it is already possible to envisage their existence. There is nothing absurd in believing that for mankind there will come a time when the difference between its mathematics and those of to-day will be as great as that between living matter and the inorganic world.

At the other end of the scale of theoretical knowledge, physical theory allows us for the first time to catch a glimpse of its real nature, no longer, that is, as a mere abstract result of the partial reduction of experience to mathematical terms, but as a determined effort to build up a rigorous doctrine of realities which can be observed and subjected to experiment, rather as mathematics is succeeding in establishing itself as a rigorous theory of realities which may be represented as having extension and number. We do not yet realize how revolutionary is the intellectual phenomenon constituted by the first theoretical adumbrations underlying the work of an Einstein, a Dirac and the great cosmological physicists of our time, Eddington for instance. There is arising a clearer awareness of the correlation between the analysis the physicist makes of his own specific activity and the discovery of certain of the constituent structures of cosmic being. At the level of the sentient and the cosmic, theoretical physics is well on the way to doing what mathematics does at the level of the imaginable and of purely quantitative extension.

Hence the theoretical sciences seem to be developing along rather new lines and to be roughly grouped in the three orders of Logic, Mathematics and Theoretical Physics, thus allowing us to hope that the powers of the intellect will be renewed and that the human reason will acquire a firmer grasp of its own nature. The time has now gone when Descartes could observe in the first outlines of modern mathematics the justification for granting a greater autonomy to reason than had hitherto characterized mental life. A far more extensive order of results is now establishing itself, and the mind will only have to reflect upon these in order to discover in them the beginnings of a theory of reason more powerful and more coherent than that exemplified by the philosophy of the past three centuries.

This possibility of an increase in the power and depth of our awareness has one drawback. However well-established it may be, the system of scientific reasoning which we now see in course of elaboration is only a partial development of human reason and still more, only a partial development of the mind. It requires to be accompanied by a whole series of complementary developments. The human mind seems to be so made that when scientific thought becomes conscious of its power in the realm of theory, it tends to behave like an over-vigorous plant, smothering the other possibilities of germination and growth that lie around it. The intellectual growth which is now taking form brings with it the risk of a hypertrophy of a certain type of reasoning. Both from the point of view of the spiritual consequences for minds spellbound by this increased potential of knowledge, and from the practical standpoint of the repercussions in men's lives if these are to be modelled too closely on this type of reasoning, the risk is serious and calls for a powerful effort on the part of those minds who are solicitous for the whole estate of man and the maintenance of a simultaneous unfolding of all his various potentialities.

These are for the moment the principal aspects of the achievements of science and their more immediate human implications. All these achievements which are both answers to questions and grounds for further inquiry, bring with them the prospect of a wonderful development of man's being on the one hand, and on the other, definite risks which it would nevertheless be false to believe are the forerunners of a future which is fated to be one of terror. In fact, if we limited ourselves to considering the present state of scientific knowledge for its own sake alone, we should readily decide in favour of an optimistic view. Even when the deficiencies of our intellect are taken into account, the chances of a human catastrophe occurring accidentally as the result of some error or some outbreak of mass hysteria, appear slight indeed and are offset by the permanent possibility of a return to normal which is of the very nature of intellect. In this connection the method of progress by trial and error would seem to promise reasonably good results.

The human element in Science and the decisive importance of the Political context

The drama of the situation lies in the fact that we cannot be content with such a simple view of things nor consider that the future of humanity in possession of scientific knowledge depends only on the specific conditions of this scientific advance itself. Science operates in a wider human context. Its power to inspire both joy and fear derives chiefly from the state of affairs presented by this context. If humanity to-day is full of fear, it is because the immediate horizon of science is a *political* one, whose grave implications for mankind it seems difficult to minimize. The conquest of atomic energy would have given rise to nothing but enthusiasm were not mankind divided by imperialisms in daily danger of going to war one against the other. No fact could be more obvious; there are others of a similar kind. If we did not know that man is liable to attacks of tyrannical frenzy, we should have little to fear when we consider the production of machinery which will make it possible to rationalize human existence on all its planes. It is only the prospect of a rational tyranny which gives us pause. Viewed from this angle there is something heart-rending about the paradox of man's political situation. Two of its aspects should, we feel, be noted.

1. *The danger of exhaustion.* In the first place, whilst the present state of science requires the early and peaceful unification of the world, a unification which would give the supra-national community of all mankind the stability of an institution, mankind itself remains deeply divided by conflicting interests, mutual distrust and ideologies. Bitter experience of human relationships does not allow us to hope for a non-violent settlement of this present state of discord between the rival imperialisms. But to-day, the use of military force can, with the aid of science, become so intense and widespread that it may cause

universal ruin. Even if the barriers between the imperialisms are destroyed, the combatants, whether victors or vanquished, may both fall from sheer exhaustion into a state in which they are powerless to continue the present forward movement. We may see again, but now on a world-wide scale, a repetition of the state of affairs in the West after the breaching of the "limes romanus" and the influx of the barbarian peoples. Such a gigantic interruption of the rhythm of history is by no means an impossibility. It would hold up many a development and change many of our present anticipations into vain Utopias. Would it necessarily mean the end of mankind? On the contrary, it may be considered as a kind of new Middle Age, a period in which we can recover our breath and assimilate into our human nature realities which we now feel are too far in advance of the rest of our soul's powers. Thus we may experience a slow return to health, as in unconscious biological processes, leading to a more balanced deployment of our forces as we go forward on the next stage of our journey.

2. *Universality of the human race and the differentiation of societies*. This first view of the human question is nevertheless inadequate. Another possibility suggests itself. Modern science has not developed among all mankind everywhere at one and the same time. Its victorious progress and its main principles have been and remain for all practical purposes the prerogative of a particular limited group—that of Western European man. Here science is really at home. When imported elsewhere, as it has been in our own times, its role is subordinate and peripheral. India, Islam, China, Africa, and *a fortiori* the still more primitive groups, are not imbued with the same energy for research and for its practical applications as the nations of the West. Undoubtedly in some groups, the sense of the various values external to and superior to those of science causes them to look down on this immense effort, the burden of which they see undertaken by

others. But the truth contained in this attitude of disdain is a very limited one. Science by its very existence effectively comes to grips with all human reality, deals with the life of all groups and handles them in the same kind of way in which the nervous system in an organism regulates the functioning of the organs and tissues from which it has become differentiated. Whether we like it or not, that section of mankind which has made scientific research its own preserve, is destined to exercise control over that organism which our world in fact is. In relation to it, the other sections, like the less advanced segments in an organic development, are destined to play the part of subordinate bodies, whose lot it is to do the heavy work, which precedes the nobler activities of the whole organism.

Further, the manner in which mankind is actually divided in this respect, seems to lead to the conclusion that this differentiation is, at least in essentials, an irrevocable fact. The masses have backed their choices. As far as the affairs of this world are concerned, Western man seems too far ahead to be overtaken. Yet the paradox remains that, given the biological aspect of man's nature, such a situation appears normal, and yet at the same time unacceptable in view of the spiritual aspirations of the human conscience. For if science is, as we believe, an authentic human value, then it must be shared *uniformally* by all mankind, and the differentiation must gradually disappear. There is a danger that it will not in fact disappear at all. If that is the case, then within a political unification of the world, this differentiation will perpetuate civil strife between the group of men who have reached an adult status with the aid of science, and those who are still compelled to remain minors and who revolt because they realize what their condition is. This leads to the tragedy of oppression and its methods. To suppress this realization and the revolt to which it gives rise, is beyond the power of any technique whereby mankind can be scientifically organized. Science can never eliminate from mankind the possibility of reflexion. Nevertheless the attempt to effect this elimination may continue more or less persistently and usher in an era of scientific tyranny. We cannot hide the fact that the threat of such an era becomes daily more insistent. In the first place, it is by no means certain that Western society as a whole will move into the next phase of science. The events of recent years suggest on the contrary that there may arise a new kind of differentiation among the Western nations, and that some of them have already fallen so far behind that they can never hope to recover the ground they have lost. France to-day is beginning to reflect on a state of affairs which is tending to develop without her co-operation. Scientific energy is obviously becoming concentrated in the hands of a smaller group under whose control we are bound in part to fall. As this concentration increases, the greater will be the temptation for the privileged group to maintain the difference between itself and the rest and to dominate it both technically and spiritually.

At the worst, it is not extravagant to imagine an attempt to set up a "Brains Trust" having in its hands all the controlling levers of science and whose intention it would be to organize once and for all the subjection of the rest of mankind to these controls. Science would then order in varying degrees the internal functioning of the entire race. Such functioning is essential for the smooth running of the whole, but it is also, unfortunately, inseparable from a state of slavery. Life would then be a burden which would in no way be lightened by the individual deliverance which our nature as men always in theory makes possible.

If such were to be the future of mankind it is unlikely that the masses would remain dormant in their spiritual degradation. They would be in the terrible state of men so oppressed as to be permanently deprived of the power to react effectively against the forces that keep them under. Their revolt would be purely a matter of form and could only succeed in filling them with despair, conscious as they would be of their plight. This is already beginning to be the condition of peoples now seeking to achieve their emancipation. If we could understand this state of mind from within the situation, we might perhaps be able to realize that the fate which is theirs to-day may to-morrow be ours.

Strictly speaking it seems impossible that events are absolutely certain to develop in this manner. Nothing human is absolutely certain. In every human movement there is progress up to a given point. The neglected sides of man's being then call on him to retrace his steps. However, even when the discord between the nations has been abolished, if it ever is to be, the impetus of the revolt of the subject peoples will doubtless be the fundamental factor acting from within the situation as a brake upon the development of mankind. It will also involve the permanent risk—painful though perhaps in the long run beneficial—of the loss of all that has been gained, to say nothing of the misery of which it is both the sign and the cause. When our human condition is taken into account, it still seems likely that the history of the future will, like that of the past, be one of continual toil and uncertainty. We can be sure of nothing in that future. The great certitudes immanent in science are always exploited in unexpected ways by history. Herein lies the value of asking ourselves questions, for the value of man's decisions will be determined, in great part at least, by the quality of his reflexions.

Christian reflexion and scientific progress

This analysis is already too long, yet it has merely outlined one or two characteristics. The least we can say is that the human mind should go courageously forward and consider these things, meditating steadfastly on the grandeur of the prospect that lies before it and facing up to the facts which give the most cause for anxiety, in the knowledge that these fears must and can be overcome. Man is always able to measure up to his problems. More than ever before, this is the lesson we must draw from our knowledge of ourselves.

But is it enough for the mind of the believer to be content with this simple will to courage and lucidity of vision? We do not think so and we would like to consider, if only very superficially, the specifically religious references in our attitude to science.

In point of fact, a Christian analysis of our present problems is by no means easy and it cannot claim to reach any definite conclusions. The role that science will finally play in the working out of man's destiny is known only to God. In many respects religious meditation leads to a deeper understanding of the problems rather than to the discovery of any definitive solution. In any case, it appears easier to determine the rules we should follow in our dealings with science rather than to say precisely what its development, even from a higher standpoint, holds for the future of mankind. True, this does not dispense us from trying to puzzle out the implications involved in this development. But rather than attempt a synthesis it is better to proceed by bringing together a few lines of thought whose convergence is of greater interest than a set of too facile conclusions.

Human Science and the Divine Plan

1. From a purely human point of view the questions raised by the phenomena of our time seem to indicate that there are two types and degrees of risk in the development of science. Man's conquest of nature is an arduous task and often brings to light the dangers and the misfortunes by means of which nature herself opposes our efforts. At the natural level, each phase of progress has its drawbacks and there is no guarantee that in our desire to

discover everything and to follow up our discoveries by practical applications, we shall not in fact bring about a universal catastrophe. However, this anxiety is of secondary importance, and the drawbacks by means of which nature exacts her toll for the gifts with which she rewards our researches, seem on the whole insignificant when compared to the gifts themselves. If this were all, mankind to-day would feel more happy than ever before about its progress. On the other hand, the interaction between scientific knowledge and the problem of human interests seems to give rise to infinitely more dangerous possibilities and far graver evils. At this level the drawbacks to scientific progress seem sometimes so heavy that one may reasonably wonder whether they do not force us to revise our verdict and to view with fear and trembling the increase of man's material power.

It is remarkable to see how the most traditional Christian positions harmonize with these preliminary observations and throw added light upon them. The nature of the cosmos does involve some degree of misfortune for man. But everything in Christianity seems to invite man to have confidence in nature. This world has been created by God who has seen to it that all his creation is good. God blessed man at the first moment of his existence and gave him power over all terrestrial creatures. These fundamental purposes of God concerning man's relations with cosmic nature seem to be still operative in the present phase of man's existence, whatever may lie in the background. Science with its great power and urge to conquest is a continuation of man's vocation as regent over all creation. From a Christian standpoint it is reasonable to hope that it will not stumble suddenly upon some hidden mystery of evil in things and so bring about the total destruction of mankind. Other considerations assure us that there is nothing in scientific endeavour which goes counter to the order of the universe. Science is not, as certain interpretations suggest, a Promethean "hybris". It is a somewhat

ATTITUDE OF CHRISTIANITY

more developed and still magnificent fulfilment of the being God gave to man when he bestowed his primordial blessing upon him.

True, man is avowedly a sinner. We nevertheless have every reason to believe that it is not at the level of the fundamental relations between science and creation that man's sin has its effects. The misfortunes inherent in nature will come upon man as a punishment for sin. As we have said, nature does not yield to her conqueror in the sphere of scientific conquest itself, without exacting her toll. Yet it is not at this point that the grave consequences of man's state of sin play their essential part. It is at the level of the relations between man and man that disorder is principally found, uncontrolled appetites and continual strife. So all the achievements of civilization threaten to turn against man by providing him with more widely effective means to perpetuate this disorder in his appetites and to make his hatred produce its fruits. In our civilization science is one of these means and perhaps the most dangerous of them all, because it is the most effective on the material plane. We must point out, however, that it is associated with many other facts which also involve risks and possible evils whose reality we must not fail to recognize. In such circumstances man has always to cry out for the intervention of the power of a redeemer, if he wishes to avoid seeing his achievements themselves become the cause of a grave deterioration in the conditions under which he exists. As Christians we possess the certitude that there is available to us—and to the full measure of man's needs—the transcendent source of redemptive power. Christ's grace is given to our world.

2. Need we go any further? There is reason to think that we should, for science appears to be involved in a special manner in the fact of human sin. Man, tempted from without but also consenting freely to the temptation, has disobeyed the law of God which forbade him to eat of the tree of the knowledge of

good and evil. Does this mean that a desire for knowledge independent of any relation to God constitutes what we might call the root of man's sin? To acquire knowledge by oneself and by oneself alone in an absolute sense without taking into account either the divine order in all things or any religious dependence in man's state, is not this typical of the overweening pride of the human intellect? In any case, we can apparently observe this pride playing a not inconsiderable part in man's actual claim to knowledge. In proportion as scientific knowledge is the fruit of this exorbitant claim, is it not the essential matter of human sin and the instrument most likely to bring about man's downfall?

If science is considered from this point of view as the specific occasion of man's break with God and apparently also as a punishment for sin, is it not the most formidable factor in human civilization, the factor which will ultimately determine the course of man's history? We should only lay claim to knowledge in God's presence and, if not with fear and trembling, at least with the feelings of a son obedient to his father's commands. We know that man does not ordinarily long for knowledge in this way. What then will be the fate of mankind as it rushes blindly or proudly along in search of knowledge? The Redemption should induce men to mortify this appetite for knowledge. The principles of this ascesis are indicated in the Gospels. Perhaps then, we have not developed our Christian thought sufficiently along these lines.

But it will be objected that this is a new form of obscurantism. We do not agree. It would involve an effort to purify the mind sufficiently for it to be able to deepen its researches whilst never ceasing to be aware of God and of man's relations with him.

3. In any case science may find itself at the heart of man's destiny and this is why its existence presents such an enigma to the Christian. We know that man has been redeemed by Christ, every man, and at every level of his being. In theory then there is

no reason why science like every other human value should not find its point of equilibrium in the work of man's redemption. All our toil as Christians must be polarized by this certitude. Yet we know too that man must correspond with his divine vocation by a free choice, and that the world is a divided one. Mankind everywhere does not choose as one body the way of salvation offered it by Christ. Men also refuse grace and build their existence on the basis of this refusal.

Those who accept and those who refuse Christ both attempt to bring under their control all the wealth of human existence and its many possibilities in the field of action. But in actual fact, there are no equal shares for all. The Gospel tends to win over the humble folk and fortune's outcasts, rather than the powerful and the rich. It is true that this depends at least in part on the period of history about which we are talking. Yet it does seem to be a law of human existence that the soul finds it easier to live in God's presence when it is not too encumbered with this world's goods, and even when it is painfully lacking in them, spiritual as well as temporal though they may be.

In which direction then does science face? Does it bow before the Christian Faith in an attitude of acceptance? Or has it fallen a prey to the refusal to accept Christ? Our answer again varies according to the period we are considering. When Christianity first took root, it seems that God chose the foolish of this world to confound the wise. During the medieval period the Church was the great mother of knowledge; human and divine science seemed once and for all to have been reconciled. Later new divisions crept in, and at the present time it is impossible to say whether science yields to rather than revolts against the Cross of Christ. May we hope to abolish these divisions? In theory, there is nothing to prevent us doing so; in actual fact there is nothing to assure us that we shall succeed. It is by no means certain therefore that we shall eventually see what meanwhile we earnestly desire—

modern science continuing to develop but completely reconciled to Christianity and its power to redeem and to sanctify the human will to knowledge. We must work for this end, but we must never be scandalized or grow weary if we do not meet with success.

The present state of Science and the Christian interpretation of History

Yet the phenomenon to which we have just drawn attention requires still further consideration. In the Middle Ages the West saw a synthesis—and on the whole an admirable one—between man's claim to knowledge and the redeeming power of Christ's grace. Then the synthesis collapsed almost completely from within, and modern man is engaged in a new type of science and seldom concerns himself with the Redemption. Often even, he attempts to prevent the doctrine of the Redemption from being taught. May it not be that history is beginning to move in the direction which it seems has been marked out for it by God— towards the great struggle between the Man of Sin and God's People ? Will not the Man of Sin mysteriously relive the experience of Adam ? Will he not be essentially the man who lays claim to knowledge in a spirit of revolt? Will he not carry both his desire for knowledge and his rebellion to their furthest extremes? Christian teaching, if we meditate upon it, seems to give us good reason to think so. Will not the world of Antichrist be that of science in wilful rebellion against God and of political power exalted above all else? Is not science already moving inexorably towards a world of this kind?

Although there are doubtless no firm principles on which to base the answer to this question, many Christians instinctively reply in the affirmative. We do not do so, not so much because we think those who hold this view are wrong, but because it seems to us that to give an answer is less important than to be aware of the existence of the question, and to be willing to adopt an attitude which is not content with an *a priori* certainty that things will turn out for the worst. To the very last we must strive to deliver science from the diabolical influences which threaten it. If Christians attempted to do this, then, with God's help, nothing would prevent modern science from achieving a state of sanctification similar to that which was realized in the case of knowledge in the ancient world. Future generations may perhaps smile at the thought of our present anxieties, living, as perhaps they will, in a world provisionally at peace under the sign of the Cross.

2. Further, our knowledge of the present state of science leads us to foresee the possibilities of development over a very long period, and the likelihood of several stages which will have to be gone through. Human knowledge has not yet fully grasped what life is, nor *a fortiori* what consciousness and intellect are. There is a vast number of realities of which we still await deeper knowledge. Our science is still very elementary indeed. Mankind may have a long future before it, and the dialogue between science and grace may yet move in many different directions. It is true that we do not know whether the dialogue will reach a successful conclusion or whether mankind, by deliberately shutting God out of the field of science, will find itself in a world so radically evil that its days will be shortened. Perhaps God will not allow demoniacal forces to take possession of the deeper levels of our existence. The diabolical manipulation of matter already points the way to terrifying possibilities. What then would happen if it could influence directly life itself or the conscious psyche? Because of the elect, says the Gospel, the last days shall be shortened. Perhaps we must envisage God in his mercy bringing man's existence in time to an end before science has deployed all its powers of evil, once human research has been shown to be irremediably engaged in the pursuit of evil ends. These are undoubtedly sombre prospects, but we do not see why we should avoid facing up to them, whilst bearing in

mind that there is no reason at all to declare that they are fated to be realized.

3. In any case, it seems far too soon at present to judge that human scientific effort is moving inevitably in the direction of evil. All is far from being well with mankind, and here and there the powers of Hell emerge with singular force. Yet in many respects, mankind in its immense efforts to acquire knowledge seems powerless to control certain tendencies towards evil in science, rather than bent upon organizing the world into a system based on the refusal of grace. The trouble with mankind to-day is that we experience difficulties when we are face to face with the collective nature of mankind, and with the fact that the assimilation by science of realities as living, conscious and human lags behind their assimilation as purely material phenomena. In spite of the errors which keep this unfortunate state of affairs in being, mankind continues on the whole to face up to its destiny in a spirit of good will which is singularly impressive although perhaps not particularly enlightened. Doubtless science in its forward movement is insufficiently alive to the fact that there is a divine pole in relation to which man's actions must be regulated. It is perhaps a case of ignorance rather than deliberate pride and conscious rebellion. In a sense mankind seems hitherto to have been foolish rather than intentionally sinful, and it has made pathetic efforts to rediscover the way to that full knowledge of the good whose secret is hidden from it because it does not acknowledge Christ. May not God once again show mercy towards us who 'know not what we do', and convert to himself a generation whose greatness lies in its undisguised avowal of the gravity of its distress? Should not true Christian wisdom, which is the wisdom of the heart, have confidence in all these efforts of mankind to re-establish the wisdom which should inspire all scientific research, and help it to find its true place in the affairs of men?

4. True, this demands a further effort of Christian thought, for if we consider again the divorce which for the past few centuries has divided scientific research from the religious interpretation of the universe it is by no means certain that all the wrongs are obviously on the side of man's claim to scientific knowledge. It would be naive to pretend that the concupiscence of the eyes and the pride of life have not in fact played a large part in many of the mind's efforts to acquire knowledge. But it would be unjust to see only these causes at work. In many cases, there exists between science and religious truth a barrier of misunderstanding for which religious thought is not entirely without blame, and which it alone, in any case, can overthrow. The mind in love with God must also be able to assume into the process of its own growth, all the valid acquisitions of human knowledge. At the present moment, we cannot say that it does this with complete success or sufficiently obviously. There is work to be done. It requires an effort which will often be hard to maintain and will call for delicate adjustments. But the urgency of the task is more keenly realized as the Christian conscience learns, at this turning point in history, to count more upon God's mercy than upon his wrath.

Date Due

FEB 17 DEC 8 '39			
DEC 15 1965			
MAY 21 '97			
MAY 20 '97			